Dream Kitchen Planning

Dream Kitchen Planning

Elaine Martin Petrowski

A PERIGEE BOOK

A Perigee Book
Published by The Berkley Publishing Group
200 Madison Avenue
New York, NY 10016

First edition: March 1996

Published simultaneously in Canada

The Putnam Berkley World Wide Web site
address is http://www.berkley.com

Library of Congress Cataloging-in-Publication Data

Petrowski, Elaine Martin.
    Dream kitchen planning / Elaine Martin Petrowski. — 1st ed.
        p.   cm.
    "A Perigee Book."
    ISBN 0-399-51985-8
    1. Kitchens—Planning.   I. Title.
TX653.P46   1996
643'.3—dc20   95-24041
                                                                          CIP

Printed in the United States of America

10   9   8   7   6   5   4   3   2   1

Contents

CHAPTER 1   What's a Lifestyle Anyway?   •   *And How to Plan a Kitchen That Suits Yours*   1

CHAPTER 2   The Plan Basics   •   *The Whys and Hows of Creating a Kitchen Layout*   13

CHAPTER 3   Holding the Budget Line   •   *How to Set a Realistic Budget . . . and Stick to It*   25

CHAPTER 4   The Easy-Access Kitchen   •   *Create a User-friendly Kitchen for Everyone*   37

CHAPTER 5   Environmental Concerns   •   *Plan a Kitchen That's Kind to the Earth*   45

CHAPTER 6   Floors and Countertops   •   *Making Informed Decisions About Component Parts*   57

CHAPTER 7   Your Kitchen Sink   •   *Little Things Mean a Lot*   67

CHAPTER 8   Cabinets and Storage Details   •   *A Place for Everything and Everything in Its Place*   81

CHAPTER 9   Major Appliances   •   *Picking and Choosing the Big-Ticket Items*   95

CHAPTER 10   Finishing Touches   •   *How to Add Personality—Yours . . . Not the Designer's*   121

CHAPTER 11   Working With the Pros   •   *The Whys and Hows of Working With Design Professionals*   131

CHAPTER 12   Finale   •   *The Importance of the Kitchen in Your Home*   141

RESOURCES   144

INDEX   147

Acknowledgments

With grateful acknowledgment to every cherished friend and respected colleague in the kitchen and bath industry, who, over the years, taught me all I know about kitchen planning. Too numerous to mention individually, you know who you are.

And to dear Joe, who always knew, for sure, I would do it, even when I thought not.

CHAPTER 1

What's a Lifestyle Anyway?

*(And How to Plan a Kitchen
That Suits Yours)*

We live in the age of "instants." It's the era of Fed Ex, fast food and fax machines. Just about any commodity can be ordered and on its way to you in a matter of moments, with the exception of a new kitchen. And for good reason. The number of choices and the myriad details involved in planning a new kitchen mean that its purchase and installation can take weeks or, more likely, months to complete. In fact, it's not unusual for a kitchen project to take a year or longer from start to finish.

Many people, impatient to inhabit their new kitchen, want to rush the process. For them, time spent comparison shopping, studying photos, books and magazines, and just plain thinking about designing the space, rather than getting on with building it, seems like a waste of time. But nothing could be farther from the truth, because careful advance planning is the most crucial step you can take in order to guarantee that what you are creating is truly a great new kitchen that meets all your family's needs.

You'll be happier with the end results and enjoy the process of creating a new kitchen more if you take a new perspective on the planning process. Realize that this phase is an opportunity to fine-tune the details of your dream kitchen. It's likely you've been thinking about what you really want, and need, in your kitchen for years. Take the time now to savor the process, and you will obtain maximum results for your efforts.

Remember that what you're planning is probably the most lived-in space in your home; a room you and your family will use several times every day for years to come. It might be easier to take your time with the planning process if you think of this phase as an investment in the quality of your life. Here's a chance to create a kitchen that will be a pleasure to look at, easy to care for and decorated to suit your tastes and style, as well as safe and efficient to work in for years to come.

If you still think "giving up" all that time seems foolhardy, try viewing the planning stage as an insurance policy against one form of domestic disaster. Because planning, at least in the case of the kitchen, can eliminate the possibility of future discontent. Think of planning a new kitchen as a bit like choosing a mate. Both can be joyful, positive commitments if you make the right choice. But make a mistake in either case and you'll be obliged to live with the consequences, on a daily basis, for at least some time to come. Or be obliged to undergo yet another change.

Beginning right now, dispel the notion that "well planned" translates into "more expensive." Generally it costs no more money and may, in fact, cost less to plan a new kitchen that solves all or most of the design problems of your current one. All you invest is some extra time. So if your present kitchen is totally, or even marginally, inadequate because the work areas are bisected by the traffic flow, or the space is cramped or wasted, or the range is awkwardly crammed into a corner and the refrigerator too small, don't perpetuate the inconvenience by tearing out the old and replacing it all with a second generation of identically situated, but new, equipment. Not when a bit of planning can result in a kitchen that's tailormade to provide years of safe, convenient, comfortable use.

Keep yourself as organized as possible during the planning stages. Start by picking up an accordion file folder and a marker. With a trip to the largest magazine stand in your area every few weeks, you can pick up the current crop of home decorating and shelter magazines, as well as the special-interest titles devoted strictly and only to kitchens and baths. Snip photos of rooms and features that appeal to you. (This is no time to worry about passing along the magazines to your mother, best friend or sister.) And use the marker to circle what caught your eye. Before you add the magazines to the recycling pile, take advantage of the offers to send for free product literature and the catalogs for the items that interest you, usually found near the back. File your photo collection by category: cabinets that suit your style, storage ideas that suit your needs, flooring patterns that catch your eye. File the product literature by category, too: appliances, flooring, cabinets, etc. Earmark another section of the folder to keep articles you clip on topics that particularly interest you—safety, lighting, kids in the kitchen. And set aside another section to keep this book handy all through the planning process. Since you'll likely be picking up laminate chips, solid-surfacing samples, ceramic tiles, pieces of flooring, fabric and wall coverings, etc., along the way, hang onto the box from your next pair of aerobics shoes and use it to stash all those bulky samples in one place.

What's a Lifestyle Anyway?

Despite the impact on the aesthetics of your new kitchen space, the most important step in the planning phase is not choosing the cabinets. (See Chapter 8, Cabinets and Storage Details, page 81.) Nor is it deciding what you can spend. (See Chapter 3, Holding the Budget Line, page 25.) The most crucial element of the planning process is zeroing in on which features, styles, appliances, materials and layout will work best for you and your family—in other words, what design professionals refer to as "defining your lifestyle." An understanding of how you use your present kitchen and how you would ideally like to use a new kitchen is mortar for the foundation of a successful design.

Simply put, defining your lifestyle is taking the time to analyze exactly how you intend to use the kitchen on a daily basis. Like any other purchase, from clothing to automobiles, a kitchen should fit your lifestyle. If you moved to Minnesota, you would quickly learn enough about the lifestyle to equip your home with an energy-efficient furnace and down quilts and maybe buy some cross-country skis. If you moved to Arizona, your lifestyle would change and your emphasis would shift to efficient, central air-conditioning; cool, cotton bed linens; and perhaps installing a swimming pool.

The same principle applies to your kitchen. Singles, newlyweds or two-career couples might want a kitchen that's sleek and easy to care for. Items such as a microwave oven; a smooth ceramic glass cooktop; an instant hot-water dispenser; a delay-start dishwasher; wipe-down, no-fuss surfaces and any other time- and work-saving devices would, in all likelihood, be top-priority features.

The young family with small children has different needs, and so could opt for different features. They might get the most from a kitchen/family-room combination with a snack bar, wipe-off cabinets with a nearly inde-structible exterior and lots of shelving that can be adjusted as the kids grow. Appliances might include a refrigerator with an in-the-door ice and water dispenser, and a microwave installed at a kid-accessible height. A secondary sink to accommodate extra helpers might suit this lifestyle. This family might also include an out-of-the-traffic-pattern niche for the family pet to eat, as well as a place to store a case of pet food and another to stash all those empty cans awaiting recycling.

When the kids are grown and gone, that same couple, now what de-mographers call "empty nesters," might remodel to create a compact kitchen that's high on style and low on maintenance. Or perhaps plan a kitchen suitable for not one but two, or even more, cooks, complete with a fireplace and a dining nook. There might be a greenhouse window to grow fresh herbs. And if there's time in their schedule to host dinner parties, a warming oven, wine cooler and butler's pantry could be top priorities now.

It's easy to see why every element of your new kitchen, from the floor plan, cabinet finish and brand of appliances, right on down to the type of hardware and the style of the faucets, should be chosen based on your lifestyle and not on the lifestyle of friends, neighbors or relatives or even on what you see in those books and magazines. By all means, use those as sources of inspiration. But adapt what you see *to meet your needs*. And re-member, every possible component of that new kitchen has a pro and con.

It's your job, via a little soul-searching, to discover what those are and then make choices that suit the requirements of your situation. Before you set foot in a kitchen dealership or a cabinetmaker's shop, before you call the architect or the contractor or tear off one inch of that old wall covering, take the time to analyze your lifestyle so you can design a kitchen that meets your needs.

Think along these lines: Do you need, or want, two ovens? Yes, if your family lives on potatoes and roasts, if you entertain a great deal or you have a large family. No, if you never bake and prepare meals primarily on the grill or in a wok. Do you need or want an island floor plan? Not if the space you have to work with is so tight you're losing ground instead of gaining convenience. Should you buy a side-by-side refrigerator? Maybe not, if you live on frozen pizza. (The freezer compartment is often too narrow to store the pizzas flat.) And pristine white cabinets are always right. Or are they? Yes, if you're in love with the look and/or have the time to keep up with the inevitable fingerprints. No, if you have three small children and allow them to own crayons, or if you host, or ever plan to host, birthday parties, Cub pack, or Brownie troop meetings.

Now that you've got the idea, it's time to begin thinking about your lifestyle. Start by answering the questions posed here. They're designed to explore all of the aspects of your new kitchen you need to think about before ordering. And encourage all the cooks in the family to participate in the process. Existing conditions that are a real nuisance for one cook may pass unnoticed by another. Jot down your answers in this book, and keep them handy throughout the planning process. The information you provide here will help clarify your needs and become the foundation of your new kitchen plan.

- How many members are in the family? _____

- Are you expecting your family to expand or your kids to leave for college or their own place in the near future?   yes ☐   no ☐

- Circle the remodeling budget range you can afford.

      under $5,000

      $6,000–$10,000

      $11,000–$15,000

      $15,000–$20,000

      $21,000 plus

- How large is the space you have to work with? _____

- Do you plan to add space?
      Yes ☐ How much? _____ No ☐

- You intend to live in this home

      1–3 years

      4–10 years

      until the kids are grown

      forever

- In addition to the usual food storage, daily meal preparation and cleanup, circle the other activities you would like to take place in your new kitchen.

      eat

         snacks breakfast lunch dinner

      bake

      plan parties, menus

      entertain

      homework

      games

      hobbies or crafts

      laundry or ironing

      talk on the telephone

watch TV

listen to music

feed pets, store pet foods

store cleaning supplies

other

- Do you or any family member have a physical limitation (poor eyesight; difficulty bending, reaching, stooping, grasping) that should impact on the kitchen design?

  yes ☐
  no ☐

If yes, elaborate: _____

_____

_____

- List at least three things about your present kitchen that you couldn't live without. (There must be something . . . the view? the morning light? an eating area?)

  1. _____
  2. _____
  3. _____
  4. _____
  5. _____

- List at least three things about your present kitchen that you'd gleefully live without.

  1. _____
  2. _____
  3. _____
  4. _____
  5. _____

- Circle any items that are not located in your present kitchen that you would like to make room for in your new kitchen.

  vacuum cleaner

  cleaning supplies

  ironing board

  laundry equipment

  pet foods

  recycling

  hobby supplies

  computer

  television

  seasonal serving pieces

  odd-sized pans

  cookbooks

  a collection

  other (specify)

- Does your kitchen receive adequate daylight?

  yes ☐

  no ☐

- How often do you plan to shop for fresh foods?

  every day

  twice a week

  once a week

  other

- How often do you plan to shop for staples?

  every day

  twice a week

once a week

every two weeks

once a month

- How many cooks normally work in your kitchen at the same time?
1, 2, more than 2

- What is your preferred cooking fuel?
all gas

all electric

gas oven, electric cooktop

gas cooktop, electric oven

halogen

magnetic induction

- Does your current kitchen contain a microwave?
yes ☐ no ☐

- If yes, who is the primary user?
adult

child

- Have you considered how you might use a microwave in your new kitchen? Circle all that apply.
reheating leftovers

defrosting

making popcorn, snacks

meal preparation

- Does your current kitchen include a dishwasher?
yes

no

If no, why not?

If yes, how often do you run it?

At what time of day?

Who loads and unloads it?

Where do you store the dishes?

- My cooking style is (circle as many as apply):
    gourmet
    roasted meats and mashed potatoes
    broiled fish and fresh tomatoes
    grill and wok
    cook large batches and freeze
    out of the package in the freezer and into the microwave
    other

- My family's eating style is:
    one at a time, grabbed as they can
    casual togetherness
    formal togetherness
    other

- My entertaining style is (circle as many as apply):
    large group
    small group
    adults and children
    adults only
    formal and elaborate
    relaxed and casual
    potluck buffets
    the kids' friends in for lunch

haphazard

nonexistent

other

- The decor of my home is:
  eclectic

  traditional

  country

  colonial

  contemporary

  craftsman

  Southwest

  other

Congratulations. You've (hopefully painlessly) begun the process of defining your lifestyle. As you make decisions and formulate your kitchen plans, keep in mind there are no right or wrong answers, no single right choice of components, because every kitchen plan is a series of compromises.

So relax and slow down a bit. Take time to consider all the options and what they mean to you and the other cooks in your family, to the function of the kitchen and to your budget. Think things through now, rather than discovering possible design solutions or product preferences *after* you've ordered or, worse yet, installed your new kitchen. And, if you find you were unable to answer some of the questions, make that your signal to do more thinking, or perhaps some comparison shopping, until you can comfortably answer those questions you skipped. And remember that the more time you put into the planning stages now, the happier you're likely to be, for years to come, with the kitchen that results.

CHAPTER 2

The Plan Basics

*(The Whys and Hows of Creating
a Kitchen Layout)*

Despite its up-to-date appearance, it's likely you stash snacks, cook holiday dinners, and wash dishes in a kitchen that's based on the lifestyle Americans led as long as 75 years ago. That was before two-career families, whose members finally find time to get dinner on the table only after dealing with the pressures of their "other jobs," became the norm rather than the exception. That was before microwave ovens, dishwashers and automatic laundry equipment became commonplace in the home. And before the importance of proper ventilation became apparent, or even necessary. That was before the television and computer invaded every room of the home, including the kitchen, to instruct, entertain and/or infuriate both adults and kids on a daily basis. That was even before the advent of frozen foods. That was before electric coffeemakers and grinders, blenders, food processors, can openers and knife sharpeners, along with a profusion of other kitchen appliances, gadgets and gizmos, were readily available, if yet invented.

Because, until as late as 1991, it's likely that whoever built your home used guidelines based on research initially conducted in the 1920s and last updated in the 1950s to create the layout for your present kitchen. And that's a best-case scenario that assumes any guidelines at all, other than the builder's bottom line, were used.

Kitchens Are Changing

Recently kitchen design and planning principles have undergone a thorough revamping. A new study, "Residential Kitchen: Planning Principles for the 1990s," conducted by members of the Department of Design, Housing and Apparel at the University of Minnesota's St. Paul campus and released in April 1991, aimed "to integrate new technologies and changing family roles into the kitchen planning process." In other words, update the planning principles for the most used room of the home and bring them into line with the lifestyle Americans lead now.

Practically applied to the average family's kitchen, that means find the ideal spot for the microwave; update lighting and ventilation requirements; expand storage capabilities and work surfaces; provide sufficient electrical outlets; make provisions for recycling, for more than one cook to share the same space, and for the appointment calendar, the telephone, television and possibly even the computer, to share the heart of the home with the family who lives there. And those are but a few of the changes that technology and the last 75 years have wrought on the design of the modern kitchen.

The study, funded by the National Kitchen & Bath Association (NKBA), a trade association made up of some 6,000 kitchen component manufacturers, distributors, dealers and designers, provided the basis for the newest generation of kitchen planning principles. The information in the study, along with additional input from professional kitchen and interior designers and space planners, forms the foundation for the NKBA's newest "Kitchen Design Guidelines," which currently consist of 40 planning criteria (referred to throughout this book and available in unabridged form from the NKBA; see Resources, page 144) that professionals incorporate into the kitchens they design in order to maximize functionality, efficiency, convenience and safety. The planning guidelines include recommendations on designing every element of the maximally functional kitchen, from passages and aisle clearances, to the amount of storage and countertop surface, traffic patterns, appliance placement and the like.

The Basic Elements

Even if geometry wasn't your strong suit back in high school, you'll need to combine an understanding of at least one geometric form, the triangle, with a working knowledge of the NKBA's universal design guidelines in order to plan a maximally functional kitchen. Because, almost without exception, the most effective kitchen designs are based on the concept of a work triangle. No matter what its shape or size, your kitchen must contain at least one work triangle, formed by the relationship of the three main appliances—sink, range and refrigerator—to each other.

To gain maximum function and efficiency, you'll need to position the three main work centers, each representing a point of the triangle, at adequately spaced points within the room. To check the spacing, and thus the efficiency, of the layout, draw a line from the center of one appliance to the center of the others to create the triangle. Now measure the length of the lines. Each should be longer than four feet but no more than nine feet. Next, add the length of the three sides together. According to the NKBA's design guidelines, if the sum of the sides is less than 12 feet, or any one leg is shorter than 4 feet, the work space within the triangle is too cramped to be functional. If the sum of the sides is more than 26 feet or any one leg is longer than 9 feet, the triangle is probably too large to be efficient.

Shape Up

Kitchens come in all sizes, price ranges, colors and decors, but only a few shapes. In fact, the vast majority fall into one of the following categories: galley, the L-shape, the U-shape or the G-shape. Unless you're building new space or willing to undertake a major remodeling project, the size and shape of the room you have available, coupled with the placement of the plumbing lines, the windows and the entrances to adjoining spaces, dictates the shape your new kitchen takes on. And like every other aspect of kitchen design, each shape has its advantages and disadvantages.

A "galley" kitchen, sometimes called a "corridor," features the work centers on two parallel walls. This type of layout is compact and minimizes steps for the cook. No matter what the shape of your kitchen, it's important to plan a design that directs the flow of household traffic around the work triangle. That's why a corridor kitchen is not the best layout—it's impossible to keep traffic out of the triangle. One suggestion from design professionals: If you must work in a corridor plan, locate the refrigerator at the end of the room nearest the eating area to minimize the traffic passing through the work area. And with a corridor layout it's especially important to carefully think through your storage needs. To gain just a bit more storage, extend the cabinetry all the way to the ceiling. Yes, you'll need a stepladder to get at what's up there, but you need to weigh that slight inconvenience against the additional storage capability. In the corridor, or in any small kitchen, investigate the possibility of "borrowing" the space between the studs to recess the storage partway. It's often feasible, in at least some sections of the kitchen, where you can then install custom-made cabinets that are a few inches deeper than stock units. And if there's space available, consider an island on casters so that it rolls out of the way when not in use. Or pull some of the cabinets out of the straight line—say out into the room at an angle. The resultant bumpout adds visual interest and forms a convenient working area for the cook's helper. Before you opt for this treatment in any kitchen, be sure the room is wide enough to allow a minimum of a 48-inch-wide clear passageway between the bumpout and the opposite wall so two cooks can pass each other without colliding, according to NKBA guidelines. If yours is a one-cook kitchen, 42 inches will suffice.

Corridor kitchens and the (unfortunate) one-wall designs found in many apartments are ideal candidates for some of the smaller, more compact European appliances. Or consider a freestanding range and a combination microwave oven and ventilation hood. Open one wall as a pass-through to the dining or family room. It adds a bit of visual interest, allows you to communicate with family members without having them in the way, and saves steps when it comes time to set and clear the dining-room table. Gain visual interest for corridor plans by choosing complementary but different finishes for the upper and lower cabinets, perhaps a different color or texture or door style.

Many kitchens run along two perpendicular walls, which results in a work area shaped like the letter L. The L-shaped layout forms a naturally compact work triangle and is ideal for rooms with a limited amount of space. L-shaped kitchens provide a clear expanse of uninterrupted counter surface and space for two cooks to work at once, as well as offer the potential for a dining area and/or island. The L-shaped layout that includes an island works well for the kitchen that's open to a family room. Here again, consider a moveable base cabinet or butcher-block-topped portable island for the sometimes two-cook kitchen. In a really big L-shaped kitchen, it's possible to create a bit of visual interest by stair-stepping the wall cabinets in varied heights.

Planning an L-shape? Pay extra careful attention to the design guidelines concerning clearances between base cabinets, islands, peninsulas and appliance doors. For smooth operations, all walkways must be at least 36 inches wide and work aisles in a one-cook kitchen must be at least 42 inches wide. If you plan a kitchen with a dining or seating area, allow 36 inches of clearance from the counter or table edge to the wall or any other obstruction behind the seating area in cases where no traffic passes behind the seated diner. If traffic does pass behind the seating area, you'll need to allow a total of 65 inches of clearance between the seating area and any wall or obstruction.

U-shaped kitchens tend to be the most efficient. The U-shaped layout is a favorite of those who prefer to cook alone and for those who aim to direct the flow of household traffic around the work areas. U-shaped plans provide an uninterrupted span of counter and, if planned correctly, can accommodate two cooks. U-shapes also offer the possibility of including a snack bar or countertop eating area.

No matter what type of kitchen you end up with, when it comes to planning an eating area, be sure to allow sufficient elbow and knee room for each diner. At a table or counter that's 30 inches high, that means a space 30 inches wide by 19 inches deep with at least 19 inches of clear knee space per diner. At a 36-inch-high counter, allow a 24-inch-wide by 15-inch-deep counter with at least 15 inches of clear knee space. And at a 42-inch-high counter, plan a 24-inch-wide by 12-inch-deep counter space and 12 inches of clear knee space. And remember, these are the recommended *minimums* to ensure diner comfort. If your sons head the lineup on the football team and your daughter's the star of the basketball team, you'll need to plan even more space.

The G-shape is actually a hybrid of the efficient U, with a short fourth leg, or peninsula, further enclosing the work area. The G-shape offers all the advantages of the U, with potential for a bit more counter and storage space. On the downside, the G-shaped kitchen can feel confining.

Both the G- and the U-shapes are ideal for two cooks. But two triangles should be incorporated then. One leg of the primary and the secondary triangles may be shared, but the two may not cross one another, according to the NKBA guidelines. If there's sufficient space, duplicate the sink or the cooktop and/or divide the cooking appliances so one cook can work at the cooktop while the other uses the oven or microwave. Aim to maximize the distance between the sink and the cooktop because this is the area that sees the most traffic during the preparation of a typical meal, especially with two cooks. If you entertain a great deal, you might want to plan this type of kitchen so that the sink faces an area where people are likely to congregate. Be sure to plan point-of-use storage in larger U's—pots and pans near the cooktop, dishes and glassware near the table or dishwasher, etc.

Fill in the Blanks

The primary work triangle is just the beginning of a functional kitchen design. You'll need to include adequate storage and countertop areas, lighting and ventilation (see Chapter 7, Your Kitchen Sink, page 67) as well as to plug into your plan the other work areas or features that you decide suit your lifestyle.

If your kitchen measures less than 150 square feet, NKBA design guidelines recommend including at least 144 inches of wall cabinet frontage occupied by cabinets that are at least 12 inches deep and a minimum of 30 inches high. Cabinets located over the refrigerator, the range or oven do not count in this total unless you outfit them with specialized devices to improve accessibility (rollouts or a stepladder). The shelves throughout the kitchen must be adjustable and at least 60 inches of cabinets must be located within 72 inches of the primary sink. In addition, the small kitchen also requires at least 156 inches of base cabinet frontage. These cabinets must be at least 21 inches deep.

Small kitchens require at least 120 inches of drawer or rollout shelf frontage. In order to count toward the total, the drawers must be at least 15 inches wide. (Thus one 15-inch-wide, four-drawer unit counts as 60 inches of drawer space.)

Kitchens over 150 square feet require proportionately more cabinetry and drawers: at least 186 inches of wall cabinet frontage, 192 inches of base cabinet frontage and a minimum of 165 inches of drawers or rollouts.

In both large and small kitchens the first 24 inches of blind corner boxes can not be counted in the total. And no matter what their size, diagonal and pie-cut wall cabinets count for a total of 24 inches, and pie-cut and lazy Susan base cabinets count for a total of 30 inches.

It's the counters topping those base cabinets that will form your work area. In kitchens under 150 square feet you'll need to plan *at least* 132 inches of usable countertop frontage in order to provide adequate elbow room for cooks, as well as for adequate landing surfaces for the range, oven, microwave and refrigerator and a loading area for the dishwasher (see Chapter 9, Major Appliances, page 95). Large kitchens require *at least* 198 inches of usable countertop frontage. And no matter what the size of the kitchen, at least 36 inches of that countertop must be a continuous sweep for the cook's preparation center. And if the shape of the kitchen and the placement of the triangle(s) dictate that two cooks stand adjacent to each other, you'll need 72 inches of uninterrupted countertop space.

Ideally, it's best to plan countertops at at least two varied heights, depending on their intended use and the height and physical abilities of the cooks. Counter heights can vary from 28 inches to 45 inches. Standard finished countertop height is 36 inches, but if you're much taller or shorter than average, say under 5 feet or over 6 feet, you may want to consider adjusting the height in at least part of the kitchen to meet your needs. Your ideal countertop height is 2–3 inches below the height of your flexed elbow for a standup work surface and 5–6 inches below for a baking center. Wherever possible, radiuses or rounded corners on countertop edges add a level of comfort and safety for all.

Of Note: According to a 1991 University of Minnesota study, the average kitchen has an area of 175.5 square feet.

Keep your eyes open for interesting alternatives in the magazines during the planning phase of a kitchen remodel, and it's likely you'll notice an array of design options you could include in your own plan. You often won't have enough space to fit them all, but here's a list of possibilities to consider, depending on your space and on those lifestyle requirements you determined earlier:

An island of your own can convert a one-cook kitchen into a two-cook kitchen, reroute traffic around the work area, provide a spot for the kids to eat snacks or guests to perch for a visit with the cook. But an island is not always an asset. Carefully consider what effect an island layout would have on passages and work areas before you decide to include one.

A **bake center** is a popular option, but it is not necessary if your idea of holiday baking is slicing up a roll of prepackaged cookie dough. However, if you regularly bake bread or have a passion for homemade pies, a bake center complete with a cool, marble countertop, bins for bulk storage of flour, plenty of rollouts for the food processor, large mixing bowls and assorted baking pans could be a wise use of about three feet of your kitchen counter allotment. Lower the height of the counter in a bake center to gain a bit of extra leverage for kneading and rolling dough.

A **planning desk** is a wise investment of a few feet of kitchen space if your family uses that room as its headquarters. Include drawer space for family files along with a bulletin or chalkboard to use as a message center and to post the family appointment calendar, transportation and practice schedules. It's a great place to locate the telephone, hang house keys, store cookbooks and recipes, plan parties and menus, and keep the grocery list, school lunch tickets and whatever else your family needs quick access to on an almost daily basis.

A **pantry** is a good addition to a kitchen, but most pantry cabinets are designed to hold canned goods. So if you and your family live on fresh vegetables, frozen entrees or takeout food and you routinely keep less than a dozen or so cans on hand, that space might be better used to hold a larger refrigerator or a microwave oven. You might also compromise by installing a narrow pantry unit alongside a recycling center or a broom closet.

Older children can fix their own munchies out of the cook's way if you include a **snack center** in your plan. Locate it between the microwave, so they can make their own popcorn, and the fridge, so they can get their own juice. Plan storage for glassware, bowls, cooking utensils, pot holders, microwaveable dishes, popcorn and a bowl of fresh fruit.

Plan a **pet area** in an out-of-the-way spot, perhaps the far side of the island or the end of the banquette. Include a nook to keep the dog or cat out from underfoot but still near the family and provide adequate storage for the most convenient size of pet food container. Some cabinet manufacturers provide pullouts to stash pet food dishes in a toekick or bottom drawer.

Don't Let All the Numbers Intimidate You

After a few attempts at a layout, you'll become more familiar with them. One hint: Create a template of the footprint of your room. Carefully measure the space available. Sketch in the location and width of doors and windows, plumbing lines and any immovable objects such as vents and fireplaces. Recheck your measurements and then ask a friend or family member to check them again for accuracy. When you're satisfied that the

outline of the room you've drawn is correct, make a stack of photocopies of the blank. Use them to doodle your ideas. You'll eliminate the time it takes to redraw the footprint for each new plan, as well as the distinct possibility of making an error when transferring measurements.

The planning stage is the time to consider many floor plan options and to move things around on paper or on the computer screen if you want to invest in a floor plan software program (see Chapter 11, Working With the Pros, page 131). It's also the ideal time to start asking everyone you know if they can recommend a design or building professional who's experienced with kitchens, to help you refine your rough floor plan into a kitchen that offers optimal efficiency.

CHAPTER 3

Holding the Budget Line

(How to Set a Realistic Budget
. . . and Stick to It)

For most homeowners, the budget dilemma for a kitchen remodeling project goes something like this: How much do we need to spend? How do we know what we can spend when we don't know what things cost? If we have $10,000 to spend, will they laugh us out of the showroom? If we tell the contractor or kitchen designer that we're willing to spend $50,000, won't she/he do everything in her/his power to make sure we spend that . . . and more? Exactly how much *does* a new kitchen cost, anyway?

These aren't easy questions to answer because the final price tag attached to any new kitchen depends on a number of variables, but careful planning does allow you to take firm control over at least some of them. Establishing a realistic figure for what a kitchen remodel costs is not a simple task, but it can be done. And it should be done before you begin measuring, shopping and writing your wish list.

Where the Numbers Come From

The National Kitchen and Bath Association conducts an annual survey of its members to track current trends and to determine the cost of the average total kitchen remodel in the U.S. For the last five years, that figure has consistently hovered close to the $20,000 mark. The 1994 figure, $17,360, is an average cost for all the kitchens remodeled by the approximately 2,000 firms participating in the survey. Since the average is the sum of the cost of all the remodels included in the survey divided by the total number of jobs reported, there are $8,000 and $10,000 remodels along with $20,000 kitchens and $40,000 projects.

The trade magazine *Remodeling* conducts an annual Costs vs. Value report to determine the average return on investment for more than a dozen popular remodeling projects, including both a major and a minor kitchen remodel. The editors use remodeling industry estimating manuals and software to compile the construction costs for the projects. Next, the figures are mailed to realtors in 60 cities to see how much return on investment can be expected in their cities. Their responses are used to calculate the cost of the remodel versus the return to the homeowners at the time the home is sold.

The return on investment for a minor kitchen remodel (refinish cabinets, install a new energy-efficient oven and cooktop, laminate countertops, cabinet hardware, wall covering, resilient flooring and repaint) which in 1994–1995 cost an *average* of $5,835, returned an average of 104%. In other words, for every $100 spent, expect to recoup an average of $104 back if you sell your home within one year. Expect even more than the *average* if you live in a hot real estate market such as Westchester County, NY (129%), Boston (109%), Atlanta (130%), Chicago (138%) or New

Orleans (122%). If you live in Baltimore (70%), Wilmington, DE (79%), or Austin, TX (71%), it's likely that your return could be less than the national average.

A major remodel is defined by *Remodeling* as updating an outmoded 200-square-foot kitchen with a functional layout that includes 30 linear feet of cabinets and counter space including a 3-by-5-foot island executed with mid-priced cabinets, laminate countertops, energy-efficient oven, cooktop and ventilation, microwave, dishwasher, disposer, and custom lighting along with new resilient flooring and wallcovering. According to *Remodeling*'s 1994–1995 Cost vs. Value report, the *average* national cost for such a remodel is $17,170. The national average return on investment is 95% for a major remodel and can climb well over 100% in markets such as San Francisco (137%), Seattle (138%), Denver (109%), Dallas (120%) and Kansas City (102%), to name just a few. Realtors in other cities, such as Boston (87%), Knoxville, TN (73%), and Des Moines (60%) reported lower returns on investments.

The condition of the real estate market in your area and how long you intend to stay in your present home have a lot to do with how much you might want to spend, and thus to recoup on your remodeling investment, at least within the first few years. But there are many other factors to consider.

How Much Can You Spend?

Are you just starting out in your first home, a handyman special you needed to empty the piggy banks to scrounge up the down payment for? You might need to consider every cost-cutting measure in the book.

On the other hand, have you just gone back to being a two-salary, two-job family who needs a convenient, easy-to-maintain space to help uncomplicate your hectic life? Or are you in the position to refinance your mortgage and take advantage of some of the equity you've built up to make improvements? Perhaps your budget might be in the $20,000–$25,000 range.

Did you just win the lottery? Inherit a tidy sum? Sell off your second home? Or perhaps you've waited years to remodel, the kids are out of college and now the sky is the limit. At the higher end of the price spectrum, it's possible to spend $40,000–$50,000 or more on a major tear-it-all-out-and-start-over remodeling project.

How Much Are You Willing to Compromise?

A new kitchen is always the result of a series of compromises. Which color? What brand? What style? And, most important to many people, how much? How much you are willing to compromise, on what items, directly impacts the final cost of your new kitchen, because each and every component of a new kitchen is available in a wide range of prices. It's possible to find a faucet for $40 or to pay $400 or more. Select flooring for $2 per square foot, or spend $52 per square foot. Spend $5,000, $15,000 or even $50,000 on cabinetry. The same situation applies to every component that makes up a new kitchen, from the lighting fixtures to the flooring, the appliances to the windows. It stands to reason that if you insist on all top-of-the-line components—natural stone countertops, custom, hand-painted ceramic tiles, every bell and whistle on every appliance that exists, elaborate moldings and cabinetry custom-made from rare wood—the resultant price tag on your finished kitchen will be high.

As a broad guideline, you can expect to spend:

$2,000–$3,000 for a cosmetic facelift, with no new cabinets, structural, plumbing or electrical changes. You can change laminate countertops, purchase perhaps one or two new appliances and replace flooring, paint and wall covering.

$4,000–$7,000 to cover the purchase and installation of new low-end stock cabinetry, laminate countertops with a standard 4-inch backsplash, and install all new basic model appliances, vinyl flooring, paint and wall covering with few, if any, structural, electrical or plumbing changes.

$8,000–$10,000 to include all of the above, and perhaps some minor structural changes, such as adding a new window or relocating a doorway.

Floors might be hardwood or ceramic, and some upgraded appliance added.

$11,000–$20,000 to purchase all of the above in a medium-quality grade of material and perhaps more elaborate structural changes, such as skylights, a bay window and all deluxe appliance features, semi-custom cabinetry, interior fittings, decorative edge treatments on countertops, etc.

$25,000 and on up to buy deluxe appliances, multiple sinks, solid-surfacing countertops and custom cabinets along with some major structural changes, such as relocating plumbing and electrical, and erecting a small bump-out addition.

What Are Your Spending Priorities?

Here again, a glance back at the entries on your lifestyle questionnaire helps to clarify your priorities. When you've noted your top reasons for remodeling or building a new kitchen, it's easier to see where it's best for you to invest your money. For example, the serious single cook might not care if the kitchen is lined with stock or custom cabinets, or has a wood, vinyl or ceramic tile floor, so long as he has two top-of-the-line electric ovens, efficient ventilation, plenty of pot storage and a gas cooktop. The two-career couple with young children, on the other hand, might put most of their dollars into expanding the kitchen space to include laundry facilities, a central planning desk with message center, a large refrigerator and pantry that allows them to cut out several trips to the supermarket each week, and a top-of-the-line combination convection/microwave oven so they can enjoy home-cooked but quickly prepared meals with the family at the end of the day.

How Much Are You Able (or Willing) to Shop Around?

If comparison shopping sounds like it's time-consuming, you're right. It is. Which is why those who take advantage of one-stop shopping, through a dealership or contractor who supplies everything for the new kitchen, pay a premium. (See Chapter 11, Working With the Pros, page 131.) Convenience carries a price too.

To familiarize yourself with the cost of the various components of a new kitchen, browse through some of the many magazines you'll find on remodeling, decorating and related topics. Be sure to read the articles that provide figures on the cost of the projects shown. But don't be misled. Note that some offer a price tag for the kitchen remodel, but eliminate a number of items, such as the labor, lighting, flooring, etc.

Here's where the time you spend window-shopping the local kitchen cabinet dealers, flooring, ceramic tile, lighting, appliance and other showrooms pays off. You'll not only acquaint yourself with what product lines they offer, you'll also begin to get a clear picture of how much various products and different brands cost.

How Much Will You Pay for Labor?

Labor costs vary widely from market to market. If you live in a major metropolitan area, where even the deliveries must be coordinated and scheduled with the building super, no one need tell you about the high cost of labor.

Growing cities or towns, for all their positive features of a burgeoning population, i.e., a building boom and a strong economy, also feature higher labor costs. It's the economic principle of supply and demand at work.

No matter where you live, it always pays to shop around for suppliers and contractors, as well as products. In an effort to save money, you might be tempted to act as your own general contractor. That means you are the one to gather and evaluate bids from not one but several cabinet installers, carpenters, drywallers, electricians, plumbers, masons, countertop fabricators, painters, wallpaper hangers, etc. You'll need to set aside time to shop for raw materials, schedule deliveries, apply for permits, oversee construction, arrange for permit inspections and generally supervise the project. Yes, subcontracting your own remodeling job can save money. But it is a time-consuming, challenging job that requires organizational ability, patience, construction knowledge, patience, tact, a will of iron, patience, and nerves of steel. (Have we mentioned patience?) Subcontracting a major kitchen remodel can *not* be done successfully in the small chinks of time between running a corporation or even managing a small business or the typical busy family. It is a full-time job that lasts for the duration of the project. More appropriate ways to save money on a remodeling project are covered at the end of this chapter.

Are You Planning Structural Changes?

What may seem like major structural work to the uninitiated is no big deal for the experienced do-it-yourselfer or professional remodeling contractor or kitchen and bath installer. Moving a doorway or replacing a window with one of the same size or relocating the sink along the same wall are, in most cases, considered minor structural changes. On the other hand, if your plans call for a room addition, or a bump-out, switching the location of the kitchen and the dining room, adding a fireplace or raising the roof and installing skylights, you are now in the realm of major structural changes. Obviously, major changes to the structure of your home will add considerably to the amount of material used, the length of time the project requires, the labor involved, and, consequently, the amount of money you're going to spend.

Often, unavoidable and totally unforeseen circumstances such as repairs necessary to correct previous faulty workmanship or to repair rot, water, carpenter ant or termite damage can add considerably to the original estimated cost. Be prepared. Count on running into at least one snag. To avoid a real cash emergency, factor in an additional cushion (an absolute minimum of 10% of your final estimated cost, but better yet, plan on 20% of that figure) to cover the inevitable and unexpected eventualities you can be sure *will* crop up.

How Much Planning Are You Willing to Do?

If you become absolutely obsessive about your kitchen plan and cross all the t's, dot all the i's, and make all your major decisions before the first nail is driven, it's likely you'll save money. Because thorough planning generally translates into fewer last-minute adjustments (change orders, in construction parlance) during the actual remodel. And that means less time and therefore less money, less waiting for the finished project and less frustration on everyone's part.

Where Not to Skimp

There are certain areas where it doesn't pay to try to save money on a kitchen remodel. First and foremost is the **design or layout of the space,** which affects function for the life of the room. A professional kitchen designer, space planner or interior designer (see Resources and Chapter 11, Working With the Pros, page 131) experienced in kitchen planning, may see a solution to a design problem that never occurred to you. It might be foolhardy to forego moving that doorway or window to save a few hundred dollars in exchange for the function you might gain. A good professional designer could tell you for sure.

If your budget is stretched to the point that hiring a professional designer to oversee the entire project is out of the question, at the very least seek out a professional to review the plan you've developed. Or, for a set, mutually agreed-upon fee, generally ranging anywhere from $500–$2,000, many independent designers will work on a design-only basis. They will produce plans and elevations that you can then take to remodeling contractors to implement. Have your plan finalized *before* you ask contractors for a bid or order any components.

The **appliances** are the real workhorses of your new kitchen. The refrigerator is never turned off. The microwave could conceivably be used a dozen times in one day. When it comes to the appliances, buy the best you can afford (see Chapter 9, Major Appliances, page 95). Often, the more expensive units are engineered so they use less energy and thus cost less to run, which means it is possible to actually recoup the additional cost of the higher-priced model in savings on your energy bills over their expected lifetime.

The **workmanship.** It's not necessarily wise to take the lowest bid that comes in the door. In fact, regard any bids that are substantially (say 25%) less than all the other bids you've asked for (you did get at least three?) as suspect.

Of Note: Don't waste your time getting bids too early in the planning process. Finalize your plans and specifications first, so that you compare kitchen to kitchen when you do call for bids. Ideally, you'll provide each contractor with the exact same set of specifications. The more precise you can be, the closer the estimate will be to the actual finished cost. For example, if you can ask for a brand X greenhouse window in such and such a size, laminate countertops with full height backsplash (color to be decided) and decorative edge treatment, the installation of specific appliances by model and numbers, etc., you will obtain the most realistic bid.

Possible Places to Cut Costs

There are any number of ways to make sure you don't cross over whatever budget line you do set.

Stock cabinetry is generally much less costly than custom-made cabinets. (See Chapter 8, Cabinets and Storage Details, page 81.) Or order from a manufacturer who offers a semi-custom line, in which only the few units that are not standard size need to be custom-built for your kitchen. You'll find multitudinous attractive, functional styles to choose from. You will not necessarily be compromising on the quality of the cabinets, but rather taking advantage of the stock manufacturer's economy of scale.

Opt for **ceramic tile or laminate countertops** with decorative edge treatment in all or part of the kitchen as opposed to costly natural granite or solid-surfacing materials.

Look for specials and sales on component parts. Merchants offer seasonal discounts on **paint, wall covering, flooring,** etc. The time of year when you remodel may affect the cost of your kitchen. In most areas, winter is traditionally the slowest season for remodeling contractors, so you might receive slightly lower bids then at the height of the spring/summer remodeling rush. However, remember that in winter you, too, along with the kids, their friends and the cat may well be forced indoors and cooped up with the dirt, dust and the noise of remodeling. Is it worth it?

Hold off on some of your purchases until later. Install laminate countertops that can be replaced with solid surfacing later on. Reinstall that perfectly acceptable, nearly new dishwasher and/or refrigerator. Add the copper pot rack or those storage inserts in a year or so, when your wallet has somewhat recovered from the initial shock.

Do part of the work yourself. With a little coaching from a good how-to book or an experienced friend, many people find they can successfully handle the final stages of remodeling the kitchen themselves. Paint, paper, and stencil yourself and you could end up keeping a few thousand dollars in that wallet.

Do all your own planning before you start the project. Nothing adds to the bottom line faster than changes to your plan once remodeling is begun, or worse yet, when parts of the job are completed.

Try to work around established **plumbing and lighting.** If you can come up with a viable floor plan that doesn't require moving the plumbing lines, you'll save anywhere from $1,000–$2,000. Keep in mind that electrical work must be done according to code. This is not an area where it is easy to cut costs, unless you buy less expensive, decorative fixtures.

Armed with what you now know, get to work on your own budget. Here's a look at some prices to consider. It's difficult, if not nearly impossible, to decide exactly what to include in a kitchen remodel if you haven't a clue to what the individual components cost. To give you a hand in planning your budget, here's a breakdown of the items most likely to be included in a kitchen remodel. Be aware that prices may vary somewhat from market to market and are intended only as a broad guideline. A hypothetical budget for the same-sized kitchen layout at three different price points could look something like this:

Item	Low Price	Medium Price	High Price
assorted cabinets	$3,000	$8,000	$15,000+
cabinet storage inserts	$150	$600	$1,200
countertop/backsplash	$15–$20 laminate per linear foot installed	$35 ceramic tile per square foot installed	$200 granite per linear foot installed
flooring	vinyl sheet flooring $15–$20 sq.yd. uninstalled	ceramic tile $7–$10 sq.ft. uninstalled	ceramic tile $20–$30 sq.ft. uninstalled
double-bowl sink	$250	$700	$1,200
faucet(s)	$100	$300	$800
refrigerator	$700	$1,200	$3,000
cooktop	$250	$650	$2,000
oven(s)	$250	$700	$1,500
dishwasher(s)	$300	$700	$2,000
microwave	$100	$350	$1,000

Except where noted, these figures do not represent installation costs such as plans, permits and labor.

CHAPTER 4

The Easy-Access Kitchen

*(Create a User-friendly Kitchen
for Everyone)*

If you think universal access means designing a kitchen complete with rocking chairs and separate cabinets for the high-potency vitamins, think again. Accessible, or universal, design is just plain smart design. It's based on the science of ergonomics, which is the relationship between you, the tasks you must perform and the equipment you use to perform them. Accessible design requires a knowledge of your body size, strength and abilities. It incorporates your needs, based on your lifestyle. It might not require any special products, but does take a bit of extra thought and planning.

Accessible kitchen design meets everyone's needs, from those who use a wheelchair or have limited sight or mobility, to the tiniest child, eager to "help" Dad and Mom. It includes active young parents on tight schedules, and the energetic grandmother who hosts weekly, elegant dinner parties. Everybody can benefit from a kitchen designed with accessibility in mind, not just the more than 43 million Americans the government estimates are disabled in some form or another.

Again, a qualified designer is probably your best bet for helping to fine-tune your kitchen plan to ensure accessibility, for creating accessibility can affect the placement and location of large items such as appliances and storage space, on down to the light switches and electrical outlets.

Start With an Accessible Plan

Begin your planning by creating easy access to the room where the kitchen is located. Plan the transition from room to room without thresholds. Hallways and passages leading to the kitchen should be wide enough to provide easy access to all, which according to the NKBA kitchen design guidelines (see Chapter 2, The Plan Basics, page 13) means they should be a minimum of 42 inches wide and the clear width of doorways a minimum of 32 inches wide. The truly accessible kitchen includes aisles and passages that are wide enough to allow for the turning radius of a wheelchair, or for two ambulatory cooks to pass each other.

The most efficient kitchen layout is a U-shaped plan. (See Chapter 2, The Plan Basics, page 13.) All working areas are within a few steps of one another, and traffic is routed around, not through, the work area. Countertops flow continuously, which means children and those with limited mobility can scoot heavy items along the surface instead of carrying them.

No matter what shape kitchen you have to work with, strive for a design that maintains an efficient work triangle. Measure that triangle as described in Chapter 2. Keep in mind the total of the three sides of the work triangle you've created should not exceed 26 feet. And in cases where limited mobility is a primary concern, consider working within a smaller triangle to eliminate unnecessary movement. But also remember that a work triangle measuring less than a total of 12 feet will be too small and can create traffic problems.

Follow the recommended guidelines for planning adequate counter space for loading and unloading the dishwasher and refrigerator (see Chapter 9, Major Appliances, page 95) as well as to act as a landing spot for hot pots and pans removed from the range, cooktop, oven or microwave.

Add Accessible Appliances

Anyone over the age of 40 who's experienced the mysterious shrinking of type on newspapers, aspirin bottles, and cereal boxes will appreciate appliances that feature easy-to-read controls. Models with electronic touch pads are easy to operate. And for the entire family's safety, look for a cook-top with controls located at the front or to the side of the unit, not behind the burners.

Consider a magnetic induction cooktop, which transfers heat to the pot and has no open flame or hot element to contend with. The downside of induction cooking is that you may need to give up some of your old favorite cookware and purchase new, since all utensils must be magnetic and have flat bottoms to ensure contact with the surface. Install ovens and microwaves below countertop height for children and for the person who uses a wheelchair or who has limited capacity for lifting. Be aware of the location of hinges on the oven and microwave doors. Look for models that are side-hinged to allow the door to swing out of the way. It's difficult for someone with limited upper body strength, or for that matter, for someone currently experiencing a flare-up of tennis elbow or bursitis, to reach over a hot oven door to remove a heavy roasting pan.

At the sink, easily the most used appliance in the kitchen, install faucets with blade- or lever-type handles that are easy for all hands to use. Choose a faucet with a pull out hand spray that yields to gentle pressure. A good accessibility test for a faucet, and for cabinetry and other hardware, is this: If you make your hand into a fist and can still operate the levers or door handles with gentle pressure, they will accommodate small hands and stiff hands and everyone else's hands, too.

Think about installing not one but two sinks, at different heights so that everyone's needs can be accommodated. By leaving a kneehole beneath one of the sinks, you can create a spot for sitting. Be sure to encase the pipes with insulation so a seated user is not burned. According to NKBA design guidelines the knee space under any work center must be 27 inches high by 30 inches wide by 19 inches deep in order to function properly for a seated user. And specify that the sink be flush-mounted for easier cleanup.

Consider installing the dishwasher 6–18 inches off the floor for greater accessibility. It's a help for adults with back problems, as well as for those in wheelchairs, and also makes loading and unloading more efficient for busy family members.

Purchase modular refrigerator units and locate them under the counters. Or opt for a side-by-side refrigerator with ice and water dispensers in the door. For those with limited mobility, such a refrigerator eliminates a number of actions that normally would be required to get a glass of water or ice. And, because the door swing is smaller, someone with limited mobility will have an easier time getting around the doors. If small children live in or visit your home, they can help themselves to a drink without the possibility of leaving the ice out or the freezer door ajar.

Relocate the laundry to the kitchen area. Stacked units might be the ideal solution. However, these are not the best option if a child, someone confined to a wheelchair or someone with limited arm and shoulder movement needs to use them.

Cabinetry

When planning storage for a truly accessible kitchen, you'll need to take into consideration the primary cooks' physical sizes. Don't be surprised if the planning questionnaire of many professional designers includes a spot to record the height and the length of the arm's reach of the primary cooks. The goal is to put the bulk of the storage in the area between the eyes and the knees to minimize stooping and reaching. That way you can locate the items you use infrequently in the harder-to-reach highest and lowest nooks and crannies. Be sure your kitchen plan includes a sturdy stepladder to reach those higher shelves when you do want to get at the chafing dish, the punch bowl or the turkey platter.

Make sure the cabinets you pick feature quality, easy-gliding hardware and magnetic closures. And choose large, easy-grip handles. Small, round knobs are difficult for children or those with arthritic conditions to manipulate. Brightly colored, U-shaped wire or plastic pulls are easy for everyone to see and to use.

Don't skimp on the interior fittings of the cabinets. The NKBA design guidelines call for at least five storage organizing items in every kitchen to maximize function. Make digging out the waffle iron, cookie press or other odd item on the back of the shelf a thing of the past by installing roll-

out bins, adjustable shelves and deep drawers that pull forward and bring the contents to you. Eliminate the cabinet door, and you eliminate some of the motion necessary to reach what's inside. Open shelves, and again, drawers, provide the most accessible type of storage. Finally, many European manufactured cabinets can be installed at adjustable heights. This feature allows the height of the cabinets to be changed at any time without having to remodel the entire kitchen.

Surfaces

If your needs or the needs of a family member warrant, steer clear of highly reflective countertops and backsplashes, such as mirrors and high-gloss laminates that may be a problem for older eyes that are sensitive to glare or may cause visual confusion. Plan for contrasting colors on the countertops, cabinets and floor to make it easy to tell where one begins and the other ends.

You can install standard 36-inch-high countertops and include several concealed pullout work areas at lower levels. Or follow the recommendations in the NKBA guidelines and plan countertops installed at heights that vary from 28–35 inches above the finished floor to 36–42 inches depending on the user's height. This way those who prefer to work standing up will be as comfortable as those who like to work sitting down. Include a ceramic tile inset, or perhaps a stainless-steel surface, adjacent to the range or cooktop to provide an always-at-the-ready and easy-to-reach landing spot for hot pans.

Avoid flooring that's slippery when it gets wet, such as some ceramic tiles and stone. And plan a border of a contrasting color tile, wood or vinyl to define any changes in floor height, although such changes are best avoided if at all possible.

Lighting

About 8 adults out of 10 have some problem with eyesight by the time they reach age 60, which makes proper lighting important in the truly accessible kitchen. As we age, all of us need higher levels of light to enable our eyes to focus easily. A 50-year-old requires about one and one-half times the light level that a 20-year-old requires for reading. Plan both task-specific lighting in work areas as well as overhead, ambient light. Be sure to locate all light control switches within reach of everyone who occupies the home, which means anywhere from 15 inches to 48 inches above the finished floor. Press pad switches are easier to see and operate than the more traditional toggle. Finally, choose light, bright colors for surfaces in order to maximize the available light in any room.

Taking the time to think about ensuring accessibility during the planning stage of a project will help keep associated costs to a minimum. According to the National Association of Home Builders Research Center in Upper Marlboro, MD, adaptations for accessibility add only about 1.5%–2% to the cost of a kitchen in a new home. Costs are more variable for a remodeled kitchen, depending on the market where the job is located and the scope of the project. Many of the adaptations cost little or nothing more to include. They simply require a bit of planning.

Of Note:
Options to consider for enhancing accessibility:
cordless telephone
built-in jar opener
electric can opener
a pullout cart to transfer dishes and food
soap and/or lotion dispenser

CHAPTER 5

Environmental Concerns

(Plan a Kitchen That's
Kind to the Earth)

The environment is an issue of importance to us all. And the kitchen, the heart of the home, is the ideal place for your family members to begin their contribution to protecting that environment. Advances in technology and product improvements over the last two decades mean that every work center and appliance offers the potential to improve energy efficiency and water consumption. And certainly the kitchen, where much of the family's trash is generated, is the logical place to begin recycling efforts.

Conservative Appliances

The newest generation of appliances (see Chapter 9, Major Appliances, page 95) is more energy-efficient than previous generations because of improved insulation, gaskets, pilotless electronic ignitions, quieter pumps, etc. The National Appliance Energy Conservation Act of 1987 mandated national efficiency standards for 13 classes of residential appliances, including refrigerators, freezers, dishwashers, and laundry equipment. (Cooking equipment and dryers are exempt at this writing, but may well bear similar labels in the near future.) The black-and-yellow labels provide specific information about the estimated yearly energy cost to run the ap-

CROWLEY 95

pliance. The efficiency ratings are based on standardized tests that manufacturers are required to perform on their products. The higher the efficiency, the lower the energy use and thus the lower the operating costs, though exact costs depend on energy prices in your area. That's why it's important to study the labels and take the information into consideration when choosing appliances for your new kitchen. Just be sure to use them to compare like models. New appliances will not only use less energy, it's likely they'll save you money in the process. Annual energy savings realized for replacing 20-year-old appliances can range from over $70 per year for a freezer to about $65 per year for a refrigerator and $40 per year for a dishwasher.

The average refrigerator uses as much as one-third of the total household electricity, or anywhere from about 750–2,500 kilowatt hours per year depending on age and model. Choose, and correctly use, a separate refrigerator and freezer, each with its own compressor, and you could save energy and reduce the kilowatt-hour usage. (Here, "correctly" means the refrigerator should not be packed tightly and the freezer should.) Because cold air is heavy, it sinks. Thus, each time you open a top-mounted freezer, the cold air falls out and is replaced with room temperature air that must be rechilled. Keep the freezer full or consider a refrigerator with a pullout freezer on the bottom to help conserve energy.

The size of the refrigerator must suit your family's specific needs. Home economists currently recommend 8–10 cubic feet of refrigerator capacity for the first two family members and 1 cubic foot for each additional person. Add another 2 cubic feet for entertaining. Analyze your family's eating and shopping habits before purchasing a refrigerator and/or freezer. For example, if you have a small family, or eat many meals away from home each week, you may not really need that 25-cubic-foot model. If you host large dinner parties frequently, or survive on prepackaged frozen foods, you may need a larger model.

Some options, such as wire shelves and see-through bins, are designed to allow for quick selection, so the refrigerator door needn't be held open for a long time. Or opt for a unit with a snack center, where the most frequently used items are accessible through a small separate door that allows you to grab orange juice or milk without opening the entire refrigerator.

If possible, plan the kitchen so the refrigerator is not located in direct sunlight and is away from heat sources. If you must install it next to other appliances that heat up, such as a wall oven, range or dishwasher, add insulation between that appliance and the refrigerator. Opt for a refrigerator model with an in-the-door ice and water dispenser and save water (because the faucet isn't running until the water is cold). Using the ice dispenser eliminates the need to open the doors frequently and keeps the interior temperature more stable. Clean the area (refer to your manual) around the condenser several times a year to insure efficient operation, and maintain a tight seal by keeping the gaskets clean. If you opt for a manual or partially automatic refrigerator, don't let more than $1/4$ inch of frost build up. It acts as insulation and makes the refrigerator use more energy to maintain the correct temperature levels.

Finally, be sure to dispose of your old refrigerator at an approved site that recycles the freon and the metal. The Environmental Protection Agency now requires that the chlorofluorocarbons in air conditioners, refrigerators and freezers be recaptured and recycled, not released into the atmosphere. This task falls to whoever disposes of the appliance, usually a scrap metal dealer. Those who flaunt the law face fines of $25,000 per incident.

Generally the scenario goes something like this. You haul the old fridge, and for safety's sake, its previously-detached-by-you door, out to the curb for bulk trash pickup. Or turn it over to the contractor who's remodeling your kitchen or to the appliance dealer who sold you your new fridge. Next stop is a dump, which may well charge a drop-off fee. From there, the appliances are delivered to a scrap dealer, who will remove a variety of components, such as the motor and compressors, oil, copper tubing and wiring, extract the CFC refrigerant chemicals for separate recycling and take the steel boxes (the average refrigerator supplies 104 pounds of steel) to a metal shredder. Since the manufacture of all CFCs will shortly be banned, the used CFCs are much in demand and are cleaned and recycled to be used in the repair of existing refrigerators and automobile air-conditioning systems.

The appliance boxes are crushed and baled for shipment to a metal shredding facility, where they are converted into fist-sized pieces of scrap. These are then sold to steel mills to be processed and remelted to manufacture new products.

Save Water and Energy

According to a University of Ohio study, the average dishwasher uses 9.9 gallons of water, substantially less than the 15.7 gallons required for washing the same number of dishes by hand. At an estimated one load per day, that's a savings of more than 2,000 gallons of water per year. So don't exclude a dishwasher from your new kitchen in an effort to save water. Keep in mind that 80% of the cost of running the dishwasher is spent on heating the water. If the distance to the water heater is long, it may pay to insulate the pipes en route. Or pick a model with an inline water heater that heats and maintains water from the cold water lines to the 140 degrees many dishwasher manufacturers recommend.

A dishwasher with variable cycles enables you to shorten the wash time if the dishes are only lightly soiled. To maximize any dishwasher's capabilities, avoid pre-rinsing, which uses more water, by choosing a machine that eliminates the need. Load your dishwasher properly and wash only full loads. An air-dry option can save energy over a standard, electrical element drying. Many models have both options.

If you choose a dishwasher with additional insulation, it will deaden noise and retain even more heat. And remember that a delay-start cycle allows you to operate the appliance at off-peak power demand hours, as well as off-peak water demand hours within your household, such as late at night while the family sleeps.

To optimize water savings, choose a flow-restricted faucet for the sink that limits the flow of water through the faucet to 2.5 gallons a minute or less, which is now required by code. Or install an automatic faucet, like the ones you've seen in airport and restaurant restrooms, which allows water to run only when an object, such as a pot, a dish or your hand, breaks the infrared light beam that controls the water flow.

Your cooking style, as well as energy efficiency, will influence your choice of cooking appliances. (See Chapter 9, Major Appliances, page 95.) Gas ranges feature instantaneous control, but only about 45% of the heat generated is directed to the cooking surface. Electronic ignition cuts down on the usage, and thus the cost, of gas. Electric ranges transfer heat to food more efficiently, but are more difficult to control. If you do opt for an electric cooking appliance, look for one with many narrow coils and large, sealed drip pans that are easy to clean. No matter which cooking fuel you choose, a microwave oven offers an energy-efficient alternative for preparing many foods.

Light the Way

Maximize the natural light your kitchen gets with larger windows and skylights. Plan for the total window/skylight allotment to be equal to at least 10% of the total square footage of the kitchen (e.g. 15 square feet of window would be the *minimum* in a 150-square-foot kitchen, according to the NKBA's design guidelines). Choose the most energy-efficient, low-E, argon-gas filled glass for the windows, and then "recycle" the available light by including lighter, or even white, surfaces, that reflect light rather than absorb it as dark finishes and surfaces do.

Electric lighting is most efficiently provided by compact fluorescent bulbs. Although compact fluorescents cost from $18–$28 each, as compared to their $2–$3 incandescent counterparts, compacts last ten times as long and use one-quarter of the energy of regular light bulbs. In fact, compact fluorescents use so little energy, they pay you back for their cost in less than two years. And compact fluorescents fit into regular sockets. Best of all, they no longer cast that eerie blue-green light you're probably familiar with from old-fashioned fluorescents. Improvements in lighting technology include electronic ballasts that allow the new fluorescents to flick on instantly, too.

For Earth's Sake

As of September 1991, a total of 33 states and the District of Columbia had enacted legislation requiring municipalities or local governments to pass mandatory recycling ordinances. At the end of the 1980s there were about 600 curbside recycling programs nationwide. By 1995, there were more than 6,000 in addition to thousands more drop-off, buy-back, commercial and office recycling programs. Which means that more families now participate in "source separation," i.e., rinsing and sometimes de-labeling glass, metal, and plastic containers, as well as collecting and separating newspapers, junk mail, cardboard and magazines. This separated trash is periodically collected, or sometimes personally transported, to the local recycling depot and then redistributed for reprocessing into raw materials so it can be used again by manufacturers. In order to participate fully in your area's recycling program, you need to develop a system to store those bottles, papers and cans until collection day. Why not locate your recycling collection point in the kitchen where much of the recyclables are generated and everyone in the family can participate?

The first step toward incorporating recycling into your new kitchen design is to determine the exact specifications for recycling where you live. Some towns recycle glass, paper, plastic and metal. Others take no plastic. Some programs require that glass be separated by color, newspapers be separated from magazines, and aluminum from other metals, while others allow commingling. There's no point in planning your new kitchen recycling center with three bins if, in fact, you'll need four or even five. As a bare-bones minimum, no matter where you live, the latest NKBA recommended guidelines for kitchen design call for at least two waste receptacles: one for garbage and one for recyclables.

Next, determine if your local program provides regular curbside pickup. If not, you'll need to start recycling in the kitchen and then move those items to a second collection point in your home where you store larger amounts between trips to the recycling center.

Only after you've determined recycling specifications in your area can you begin allocating space. The array of available options and configurations to choose from is constantly expanding as cabinet and hardware manufacturers respond to recycling needs.

In kitchens of less than 150 square feet, where space is at a real premium, plan to use a single 15-inch-wide base door cabinet, preferably located next to or near the sink. The cabinet should include a rollout shelf that's attached to the door so that when the door is opened, the bins are brought forward to you. Outfit the cabinet with two bins, placed one behind the other. Use one bin for nonrecyclable trash and the second for re-cyclables. Or specify a single tall, 15-to-18-inch-wide cabinet in which you can stack two waste bins. Use any additional space at the bottom of the cabinet for a drawer to hold newspapers for recycling. For ease of use by everyone in the family, plan a center that doesn't require lifting the full containers, but rather allows them to be pulled forward laterally to remove and empty them.

If the kitchen is a bit larger and you have more space available, opt for a 30-inch-wide cabinet with two doors and expand your sorting capabilities by maintaining three or four bins, perhaps one each for wet trash, glass, plastic and metals. Single, double, triple and quadruple containers are available in side-by-side, front-to-back or revolving configurations. Before you purchase any interior fittings, check with your kitchen designer or the plumber to be sure the fittings won't interfere with the pipes and drains under the sink, if that's where you plan to house the unit.

A sink that incorporates a waste chute that empties directly into a bin for removal or composting later is also a possibility. Below the chute there's space for two pullout bins for sorting cans and bottles or noncompostable trash. Consider allotting a bottom drawer to stash newspapers, or if your kitchen is to be built with custom cabinets, ask the cabinetmaker to include a deep drawer to accommodate several days' worth of papers. But don't make it so deep that only the strongest family members will be able to lift the papers out when the drawer is filled, especially if you expect the kids to help.

If you have unlimited space, plan a recycling pantry. Not only will you be able to consolidate everything in one place but you can customize bins, racks and partitions to your family's needs. If possible, locate the recycling pantry near the entrance to the garage or the basement or the back door to minimize the effort required to get your stash of trash out to the curb or into the car for removal. If recycling is truly the bane of your existence, investigate the possibility of installing a chute under the sink, in the pantry, or from an island, that leads directly to bins located in the basement.

Back to Nature

Once you've planned all you can mechanically do to facilitate recycling in your new kitchen, consider making provisions for a compost pile. Maintaining a compost pile can cut down enormously on the amount of wet trash your family produces. And, as an extra bonus, you can enrich your garden with the compost.

Generally, a compost pile can include all fruit or vegetable peels, seeds and pods as well as coffee and tea and nuts. Organic materials from outside the kitchen, such as grass clippings, weeds and leaves, can also be added. But do not add meat, fish or bones, or other protein sources that will attract animals.

One of the easiest ways to collect composting materials is to plan a cutout in the countertop that allows you to push waste into a stainless-steel collection bin below. stainless-steel is less likely than plastic to absorb odors. Open the drawer, remove, empty and rinse the bin.

If you're not a gardener, think about installing a food waste disposer and/or a trash compactor. But before you decide on any of these, consult local environmental groups on their recommendations for your area. In fact, your geographic location may affect your decision on whether or not these appliances are options for you, since both are banned in some areas of the country.

Food waste disposers, required for all new construction in 90 cities, including Los Angeles, Denver and Detroit, are currently still banned (for a wide variety of reasons, both related and unrelated to the disposers themselves) in others, such as New York. And if you live in a house served by a septic system as opposed to a municipal sewer, you'll need to do some sleuthing about the size of the holding tank and the leaching fields on your system before you can decide if you want your new kitchen to include a disposer. According to the National Association of Plumbing, Heating, and Cooling Contractors booklet on food waste disposers, a U.S. Public Health Service study concluded that a *properly maintained and designed septic* tank can handle the additional loads due to disposers, though tank capacity and leaching areas must be sized adequately and the tank pumped regularly.

Disposers remove pounds of waste from the home by grinding it and sending minuscule, biodegradable particles down the drain to the sewage treatment plant or into the septic system; hence the warning about septic systems. This reduces the amount of garbage that must be taken to the dump. Reducing that burden decreases landfill costs and prolongs landfill life. And the disposer reportedly doesn't put any extra burden on the sewerage treatment plant.

You'll choose between batch-feed disposer models, which start when you insert a cap into the drain and stop when you remove it, or continuous-feed models, operated via an on/off switch, usually located on the wall near the sink. Both units require a flow of cold water from the faucet during, and for a few seconds after, the grinding operation. (This water requirement is another good reason to be sure you install a flow-restricted faucet.) Larger disposer motors, extra sound deadening insulation, stainless-steel grinders, as opposed to cast nickel, add to the cost and the durability of the product.

Household trash compactors can also play a role in managing solid waste. By compressing the volume of trash via a motor-driven ramming device, the compactor allows the collection truck space to store more waste in the bin, thus reducing the need for additional trucks and additional trips to the dump. Compacted trash also saves space at the dump as well. Trash compactors are especially helpful in areas where collections are infrequent, where residents must take trash to a dump themselves or where collection fees are based on a per-bag rate.

Compactors are available in 12-, 15- and 18-inch-wide models. Select whichever size fits most easily into your kitchen, and conceal it behind a panel that matches the cabinetry. But keep in mind that the wider the unit, the more trash it can handle and thus the heavier (up to 40 pounds) the full trash bag will be. This is something to take into consideration if you have a physical limitation on lifting or you expect the kids to carry the compacted trash outside. Look for a unit that operates by means of a key so the kids can't accidentally turn it on. A trash compactor requires the use of special heavy-duty compactor bags. Because garbage remains around longer until it's compacted, you might want to consider a model with a deodorizing charcoal-filter system. If the prospect is still unpleasant to you or if you'd like to include a compactor but don't have the space in the kitchen, consider installing it in the garage.

Incorporate as many of these ideas as possible into your new kitchen plan, and you'll be well on your way to making a contribution to protecting the environment.

Of Note: Statistics reveal that each member of your family generates about 4 pounds of trash every day. To reduce your family's contribution to the 200 million tons of garbage we produce in the U.S. each year:
- *Limit the purchase of convenience foods, products in aerosol cans, and products that are packaged excessively.*
- *Use cloth napkins and hand towels instead of paper and avoid using disposable plates, cups and silverware.*
- *Use sponges or reusable rags, not paper, for cleaning.*
- *Choose refillable or reusable containers in the giant size.*
- *Remember that the metal parts of old appliances are recyclable.*
- *Avoid Styrofoam . . . it can't be recycled.*
- *Use rechargeable batteries.*

CHAPTER 6

Floors and Countertops

*(Making Informed Decisions
About Component Parts)*

The countertops in your kitchen are probably regularly doused with water and periodically subjected to stains and acids from everyday substances such as vinegar, wine and juices. Someone in your house (certainly not you) may not *always* use a cutting board, and so countertops suffer cuts and scrapes from knives as well as abrasions from grocery bags, dishes and heavy pots and pans scooted or dragged from one spot to another. The children or the grandchildren may even happily spread glue, crayons, or fingerpaint on them. And the kitchen floor suffers all of the above indignities and more, including harsh treatment from grit, sand, dirt and whatever gets dragged in. Kitchen floors and countertops stand up to some pretty rough treatment on a daily basis and yet are expected to look good and wear well for years.

Floors and countertops not only have to work hard, they need to look great and suit the style of the rest of the kitchen. As important supporting members of the decorating cast, these areas help to underscore the theme you've chosen. The type and color of the countertop material and flooring you select also affects maintenance chores over the lifetime of the kitchen.

For all these reasons it pays to install the toughest, most durable material you can afford on the counters and floor of your new kitchen. While today's surfacing options are all durable enough to stand up to everyday wear and tear for at least a decade or so, as always, the higher-priced, top-of-the-line products can be expected to perform better and maintain a like-new look for an even longer period.

Price is affected by a number of things, in addition to the cost of the raw material you select for countertops and backsplashes. The cost of labor in your particular market, the difficulty of executing the edge treatment you select, the height of the backsplash (the wall area that extends from the back edge of the countertop to the bottom edge of the wall cabinets) and the number of cutouts required for items such as sinks, recycling centers, faucets and electrical outlets will affect your bottom line in this category.

Durability and ease of maintenance should be top priorities when choosing countertops and a floor for your new kitchen. You'll also want to keep your budget in mind and choose a color and material that suits your decorating style. This all sounds like a tall order. But not when you consider all the currently available countertop options.

Plastic laminate is, by far, the most popular countertop material, used in 50% of kitchen remodels according to the 1994 NKBA Kitchen/Bathroom Industry Business Trends Survey. Laminate is the surfacing product often generically (and incorrectly) referred to as "Formica." It's actually often likened to a kind of open-faced paper sandwich made up of several layers that include brown kraft paper topped with a layer of colored or patterned paper that's topped again with a layer of melamine resin. This whole stack is bonded together under heat and high pressure. One reason laminate has been a favorite for five decades now is its price, beginning at under $10 per linear foot, installed, on up to about $50, which makes it the most cost-effective choice for countertops.

Plastic laminate is offered by Formica, as well as by Nevamar, Wilsonart and Micarta, to name but a few manufacturers, in a mind-boggling array of colors and patterns. It's even possible to design your own custom laminate pattern with up to four colors, silk-screened on as little as one sheet. Ask at a local kitchen dealership or laminate distributor for prices and details.

For an interesting and varied look, consider mixing laminate countertops with other surfacing materials. Combine laminate counters on the perimeter of the room with a center work island covered in stone or butcher block.

Or consider laminate countertops and a ceramic tile backsplash. The mix of textures helps to enliven the decor and relieves pressure on the budget. Further personalize laminate countertops by adding a decorative edge treatment in a contrasting color—for example, a green line on white—or by choosing a beveled, multicolored layered or rounded edge treatment.

If it's properly installed and maintained (always use that cutting board and clean up spills promptly with a nonabrasive cleanser), you can expect laminate to last for about a decade before it needs replacing. Laminate is manufactured in 12-foot-long sheets, so it's likely there will be several seams in a countertop. And seams are potential trouble spots in a laminate countertop, because that's where water can seep into the underlayment and cause warping or buckling. Ask your countertop supplier to be sure to plan seams in areas as far away from the sink as possible.

When deciding on a color, keep in mind that patterned laminates hide surface scratches better than solid colors and that a matte finish shows less wear than a high-gloss finish. Expect color-all-the-way-through laminates, made from layers of colored paper as opposed to the single layer of colored paper over several of brown, to cost a bit more. But a color-all-the-way-through product eliminates the dark-brown-to-black line that appears where the edges meet on regular laminates and shows wear and tear less.

Laminate floors, new to the U.S., have been used in European kitchens for quite some time. The product is sold as tongue-and-groove planking that's installed over a foamlike matting that may be placed over existing flooring. Harder than countertop-grade laminate, laminate floors require no refinishing, can be lifted and replaced in sections in the unlikely case they are damaged, and are available in a variety of faux wood species, stains and colors at about $10 per square foot installed.

Solid-surfacing materials, often generically (and incorrectly) referred to as "Corian," are manufactured by a number of companies and sold under various brand names: Corian, Avonite, Fountainhead, Gibraltar and Surell, among others. Solid-surfacing materials, used in about 33% of kitchens as reported in the 1994 NKBA Trends Survey, are available in a variety of colors or stone lookalikes for use on countertops and back-

splashes in the kitchen. These man-made polyester, acrylic, or polyester-and-acrylic products offer durability, along with good looks, at a premium price—anywhere from about $150–$200 per linear foot installed, depending on the variety of factors mentioned above.

Solid-surfacing materials, which appear to be seamless when installed properly, are offered in an ever-growing array of colors and faux-stone patterns in finishes ranging from matte to glossy. Because the material is the same color all the way through, minor damage such as nicks and scratches can be repaired by sanding and buffing. All solid-surfacing materials are non-porous, and thus stain resistant. Again, high-gloss finishes are best reserved for the backsplash and rooms that do not get the heavy use a kitchen does.

Solid-surfacing materials are tough, but not indestructible. They, too, require protection from hot pots and sharp knives. Personalize solid surfacing with more costly soft, rounded-edge treatments or inlaid designs, or strips of other material such as wood or metal, all possible for the trained fabricator to accomplish. Solid-surfacing materials are not practical for use on kitchen floors.

Since the days of ancient Rome, not many materials can beat the classic good looks and durability of **ceramic tile**, used on 31% of kitchen floors and 5% of kitchen counters according to the 1994 NKBA Trends Survey. Today's array of colors and styles is nearly endless. You'll find sizes that vary from tiny mosaics less than an inch square to huge one-foot or even two-foot squares. Many feature a natural look, such as unglazed terracotta, or mimic tumbled marble and limestone or slate. Textures vary from smooth to pebbled. Decorative borders, embedded in a field of unadorned tiles, feature motifs borrowed from nature, such as garlands of flowers, trailing ivy, animals and fish. Include your favorite to personalize your kitchen. Or select from the many precoordinated lines for a complete look.

The raw materials, production and glazing methods of different kinds of tile depend on the country of origin—chiefly the United States, Spain, Italy, Portugal or Mexico—and make some tiles more suitable than others for different applications. Dense, fine-grained porcelain tiles that have been pressed and fired at high temperatures are ideal for floors, especially in the unglazed products. Unglazed, often handmade, and thus slightly irregularly shaped clay tiles offer a rustic, warm beauty, but must be periodically resealed to keep them from absorbing the grease and oils present in every kitchen. Traditional glazed ceramic tiles, available in a range of textures and finishes that vary from matte to high gloss, require almost no attention once installed correctly.

To simplify your choice, ceramic tiles are numerically rated, by hardness, for specific uses. If you intend, for instance, to use tile on the floor, be sure to select one engineered to take the beating that floors get. High-gloss tiles, perfectly suitable for use on a backsplash or wall, will scratch and in addition could be slippery, especially when wet, if used on a floor.

Expect to pay anywhere from about $2 per square foot, uninstalled, for machine-made tiles on up to $50 or more per square foot for hand-painted, one-of-a-kind pieces created by an artist. Installation costs will depend on the complexity of the design you create with the tiles, your market area and the method the installer uses.

If you're looking for easy-to-maintain materials, ceramic tile floors maintain good looks for years with just frequent vacuuming or sweeping and a damp mop. And manufacturers now offer a wider array of colored cementitious and epoxy grouts. Some grouts must be periodically resealed with special products to prevent them from staining.

If you do opt for ceramic tiles, when they arrive check each one for chips and fine cracks as well as for uniformity of color. And be sure to order at least 10% more than you actually need so you'll have stock on hand should you need a few replacements now or at a later date.

Particularly in a large or open-plan kitchen, ceramic tile countertops tend to be somewhat noisier than some of the other countertop options. To solve the problem, balance their use with sound-absorbing materials, such as hardwood floors or wood cabinetry. And if you have severe back problems or spend hours on your feet baking bread or whipping up gourmet meals, you might want to choose one of the more resilient flooring materials.

Butcher-block countertops offer natural warmth and can be refinished from time to time to keep them looking new. They absorb kitchen clatter and are kind to knives. But butcher-block tops can warp and crack if not properly sealed and if they are exposed to excessive water, such as around the sink. Treat countertops with a salad bowl finish, a nontoxic oil formulated for kitchen use and available in woodworkers' supply shops. Prices for butcher-block countertops begin at about $50 per linear foot installed for the most popular hard maple, but prices depend somewhat on the market. You might want to consider using butcher block on only one area of the countertop as a kind of built-in cutting board.

Stainless steel offers the homeowner who is willing to pay for it an industrial-strength and spectacularly stylish countertop option that's impervious to heat and to food acids. It's ideal to mix and match with other materials, is particularly functional in the area of the range and the sink, and can blend neutrally or make its own smashing design statement.

Stainless steel is actually an alloy of carbon steel with chrome and nickel. The higher the nickel content, the brighter and more corrosion-resistant the steel. The quality of stainless-steel is measured by its thickness or gauge. The lower the gauge number, the better the grade. When it comes to finishing options, brushed stainless-steel hides scratches better than smoother finishes. Stainless-steel countertops must be fabricated by local metal workers on a job-by-job basis. Or you could opt for a stainless-steel sink with a large integral drain board. Maintain stainless-steel by rinsing with water and then wiping with a damp cloth and a dry towel. Keep in mind that large expanses of stainless-steel will add to the clatter in a busy kitchen.

Natural granite, marble, limestone, soapstone, slate and other stones are the most durable and the most deluxe surfacing materials, with the most expensive of the lot, granite, commanding prices upward of $200–$300 per linear foot, installed depending on the source and variety of the stone and the edge treatment you select. Stone prices also depend on the type, thickness and quality with most in the $175–$250 range, installed. Stone tiles are a bit less expensive than slab products. Expect long life from natural stone countertops or floors, which are even burnproof.

Be aware that some stones need to be sealed to keep them from being permanently marred by foods such as lemon and tomatoes (marble) or grease (granite) that's absorbed. Natural stone, like ceramic tile, can be hard on the feet and back and, like other hard surfaces, can help magnify noise.

Flooring also is available in a variety of choices. **Vinyl** is a soft underfoot, quiet, cost-effective flooring alternative, used in 37% of the kitchen remodels reported in the 1994 NKBA Trends Survey. Resilient flooring ranges in price from $2–$10 per square foot for install-them-yourself, 12-inch-square tiles to $10–$40 per square yard for 6-foot- or 12-foot-wide sheet goods that generally require the skills (and the fees) of a professional installer. Both products are easy to care for and are available in a wide variety of colors, patterns, grades and price ranges. Price is a good indicator of quality.

Hardwood floors, used in 28% of the kitchen remodels reported in the 1994 NKBA Trends Survey, warm up the kitchen and never go out of style. With proper care, they never need replacing, just sanding and resealing. Choose from wide or narrow planks, combine both, or create a custom border design. Investigate prefinished wood tiles that allow you to custom-design your own pattern, or consider laying wood floors on the diagonal. Many of today's wood floors are factory finished, so there's no sanding or staining required on your premises until several years down the road. To keep wood kitchen flooring in top form requires two, or better yet three, coats of polyurethane applied every few years, depending on the wear and tear your family dishes out.

Maintain wood floors with mats at the door to collect grit, frequent vacuuming and an occasional damp mopping. Uninstalled prices range from about $2 per square foot to about $20 per square foot, depending on finish, style and manufacturer.

Higher-quality vinyl products are made with the color all the way through the product, so patterns take longer to show wear. Soft underfoot vinyl "telegraphs" any imperfections from the existing floor to the surface, so make sure the underlayment is smooth. In fact, it is best to remove tne old floor before installing a new vinyl one. Vinyl floors require protection when moving or installing appliances and later on when cleaning behind the refrigerator. Higher-quality products offer better resistance to dents, cuts and tears from things such as dropped cans, furniture legs and high heels.

Manufacturers of no-wax vinyl floors recommend the use of specific cleaners. Follow the manufacturer's instructions carefully. Don't expect any vinyl floor to last a lifetime; it will need replacing after about a decade, depending again on the wear and tear you, the kids and the dog and cat can dish out and how thorough you are about upkeep.

Of Note: The standard backsplash height is 4 inches. Though more costly, you might want to consider a full-height backsplash (one that reaches from the back edge of the countertop all the way to the bottom of the wall cabinets). Whether executed in material identical with or complementary to the countertop, a full-height backsplash of laminate, solid surfacing, natural stone or ceramic tile provides a unified look, is easy to keep clean and eliminates the need to repaint or repaper during the lifetime of the kitchen.

CHAPTER 7

Your Kitchen Sink

(Little Things Mean a Lot)

It was one thin straw that broke the camel's back. And, the story goes, David slew Goliath with a single stone. The little Dutch boy held back the contents of the dike with his finger. But what do a straw, a stone and a little boy's finger have to do with kitchen planning? Simple—all are seemingly insignificant items that affected larger events. And just as one small detail had a major impact on the camel and Goliath and the inhabitants of Holland, it's often the little details of the kitchen that will have the biggest impact on its convenience and function.

With hundreds of items to mull over during the kitchen planning process, it's easy to see why choosing items such as the sink, lighting and ventilation equipment might escape careful attention. But if you're the one who cleans up from Thanksgiving dinner in a too-small sink or who uses a ventilation system that sounds like a helicopter squadron landing on the roof, or who tries to see if the dishes really *are* clean by the light of a lone, 150-watt bulb, you have firsthand experience with how the little things can add up to problems in the kitchen. That's why it's wise to give as much thought to selecting and locating the seemingly small components, such as the kitchen sink and the ventilation system, as it is to choosing large and obvious items, like the style of the cabinets or the type of countertops and flooring.

The Center of the Kitchen?

Consider this: The sink, where food, dishes and hands are washed, coffee and pasta pots are filled, and thirst is quenched, is *the most frequently used* work center in any kitchen. Although any sink will certainly fulfill the basic function of holding water, there are a number of factors to consider if you aim to maximize the function of this most important piece of kitchen equipment.

Materials

Kitchen sinks are available in a wide variety of materials. You'll need to determine which meets your functional and decorative needs, as well as your budget requirements.

Stainless steel, an alloy of carbon steel, chrome and nickel, is the most popular material for kitchen sinks. (A higher nickel content increases the corrosion- and stain-resistance.) stainless-steel is, as its name implies, stain resistant, as well as affordable. It's available in a range of sizes and styles to suit just about any decor. Keep in mind that a brushed finish shows wear and spotting less and so is easier to care for than a high-gloss mirror finish.

As with stainless-steel countertops (see Chapter 6, Floors and Countertops, page 57), when you shop for a stainless-steel sink, remember that the thicker the gauge, the heavier, the more costly, and the more durable the sink, the lower the gauge number. Thus, an 18-gauge stainless-steel sink is heavier and more durable and less likely to dent or scratch than a 20-gauge or 22-gauge.

Two cautions: If you live in an area with a high mineral content in the water, the resultant spotting will make shiny stainless-steel more difficult to keep sparkling clean, so opt for the brushed finish and more frequent cleaning. And pots, pans and dishes clanking around in a stainless-steel sink can be noisy, so be sure to ask if the sink you're considering features a sprayed-on, sound-deadening, insulation coating on the underside. If the noise is likely to bother you or a family member, it might be worth the extra dollars to move up the price ladder to a model that includes the insulation.

Prices for stainless-steel range from models as low as about $100 to near $1,000 for a triple-bowl, top-of-the-line model with a full array of accessories.

Enameled cast-iron sinks are made by pouring liquid iron into a mold that is cooled and then coated with enamel and fired in a kiln. Enameled cast iron's trademark glossy, easy-to-clean, and durable finish is available in many colors and is the sink to select if you have your heart set on cobalt blue or apple red.

Because of its weight, an enamel on cast-iron sink must be self-rimming. That means there will be about a $1/2$-inch-high lip all around the edge of the sink, which means you can't scoot crumbs and debris directly into the bowl. Just as you might suspect, enamel cast iron is durable. But if you drop a platter or heavy pot at just the right angle, the baked-on layer of color could possibly chip off, allowing the black cast iron beneath to show through. Though rare, the results are unsightly and difficult, if not impossible, to repair well. Enamel on cast-iron sinks vary in price from about $200 to $800, depending on size, color, manufacturer, shape and the accessories and styling details you select.

Solid-surfacing material sinks, such as those made of Avonite, Corian, Fountainhead, Gibraltar, Surell and Swanstone share all the characteristics of solid-surfacing material countertops, i.e., they are stain resistant, reparable, color-through and resist corrosion by household chemicals.

Remove stubborn stains from matte or semi-gloss solid surfacing with an abrasive cleaner on an abrasive pad. High-gloss finishes are not recommended for use in the kitchen. Eliminate stubborn stains with white polishing compound and a low-speed electric polisher with a wool pad.

One of the main benefits of solid-surfacing sinks is that they are rimless, seamless and built directly into a solid-surface material countertop. Sink prices range from about $500 to $1,200, somewhat higher than other types of sinks because solid-surfacing materials require specially trained fabricators to manufacture and install the sink. The larger the sink and the more elaborate the surrounding drainboard, the higher the price will be.

Nearly every major plumbingware manufacturer has recently introduced a **composite** sink material, generally molded of natural, nonporous quartz particles suspended in a resin or fiberglass. The higher the percentage of natural quartz in the mix, the tougher the sink. The new kid on the block, this composite material is available in both solid colors and granite looka-likes in matte and high-gloss finishes, and sinks generally range in price from about $300–$800. Composites may require the use of special cleaning products. They are durable, scratch- and stain-resistant, easy to clean and will not scorch. Composites are available in a number of neutral colors.

Vitreous china, the old standby in the bathroom, is not used often for kitchen sinks, because the fired clay can break if heavy objects are dropped into it. But it is possible to find European-style shallow, decorated sinks in this traditional material. If you like the glossy look of vitreous china, consider it for a second or wet-bar sink.

How Deep?

No matter which material you select, perhaps the most important feature of your new sink is its depth. The deeper the bowl, the more you can expect the sink to cost, no matter which material it's made from.

While you'll find sinks as shallow as 5 inches, 7 inches deep is the absolute minimum to consider for a functional primary sink. Standard depth is about 8 inches, but you may want to pay more for a 10-inch or deeper bowl that can handle roasters and large pasta pots with greater ease. While great for the large family or the gourmet cook, extra-depth sinks could make it difficult for the kids to reach into the bottom if you expect them to help in the kitchen. You can simply wait for them to grow tall enough, or invest in a platform stepstool.

Next, consider the shape and the configuration of the sink. The most popular shape is the rectangle, which is available in one-, two- or three-bowl configurations measuring anywhere from 12 inches to 72 inches side to side. The two-bowl—one for washing, the second for rinsing—is the most popular style. Some two-bowl models feature one high and one low bowl; some offer the same size bowls; others, one large and one small bowl. The shallow smaller bowl is used to rinse vegetables and to mount the disposer. Keep in mind that the larger the sink you choose, the less countertop space you'll end up with. And those extra few inches of countertop can become a real convenience issue in a tiny kitchen. If your kitchen is small and you must have an extra-large sink, invest in one with an optional, removable cutting board, or a built-in drainboard that channels runoff back into the sink at cleanup time, to reclaim work surface as needed.

Three-bowl sinks have made an appearance in recent years. These include a small center bowl flanked by a larger bowl on each side. The middle bowl often leads to the garbage disposal.

Consider your personal cooking and cleanup styles when deciding on the sink: For example, a large family or large batch cooking means lots of large pots and pans and necessitates a sink with at least one oversize bowl. If it's your habit to let the pots soak clean overnight, you're probably best off with a double-bowl model so there's always an empty sink available. And those who decide not to include a dishwasher in the kitchen will probably also want to include a sink that offers at least two full-sized bowls.

Shapes

In addition to the popular rectangle, you'll find octagons, squares, circles, ovals, trapezoids and just about any other shape you can draw. But some of these sink shapes are less practical than others and so ought only to be considered for second sink applications. For example, a square, 90-degree corner model is a practical and interesting way to make excellent use of awkward corners because it retains the unbroken straight run of countertop on either side as efficient work surfaces. Circles and ovals add a touch of decorative interest, but geometry being what it is, you'll never successfully wedge a large rectangular roasting pan to soak in it. You'll find secondary sinks in all of the materials mentioned above as well as specialty metals, such as brass, chrome and the like.

Of Note: About 26% of the new kitchens installed by National Kitchen & Bath Association members in 1993 included a secondary sink (bar, salad), according to the most recent NKBA trends survey.

Accessories

Just like a basic model car whose sticker price is pushed up by loading on the accessories, so too the final price tag on a new kitchen sink escalates with the addition of each convenience feature. The most popular of these include handheld sprays for rinsing dishes and the sink itself, lotion and/or soap dispensers, cutting boards, rinse baskets, a water cooler, and an instant hot water dispenser (a small electric heater installed under the sink to provide 190°F water so you don't have to wait so long for it to boil or to make instant oatmeal and cocoa). Some high-end sink models are offered with recycling chutes and integral drainboards.

You'll need to decide which accessories you want at the same time you order the sink, because the holes to mount the accessories are generally predrilled in the factory. Maximize function by selecting a faucet with an integrated pullout spray head and use the resultant free hole in the sink deck for an accessory of your choice. In addition to good looks, a gooseneck faucet offers the advantage of allowing you to fill nearly any size pot effortlessly.

Regardless of size, shape or material of construction, kitchen sinks are installed from above or below the countertop. The vast majority of sinks, regardless of price, mount from above and are known as self-rimming. With a self-rimmed installation, the lip of the sink overhangs the surface of the countertop on all sides, which can make cleanup around the sink more difficult. Self-rimming sinks are suitable for use in any type of countertop.

Undermount sinks are installed from below, so the countertop actually forms the sink rim. Spills and crumbs can be swept right into the bowl. On the downside, if you're planning laminate countertops, undermount sinks cannot be installed. There is no way to seal off the raw edge of the fiberboard beneath the laminate at the lip of the sink.

Integral sinks are fabricated of solid-surfacing material. They are built, not set, into the countertop. The countertop and the sink form a continuous smooth and seamless unit with no visible rim. However, the particulate solid-surfacing colors cannot be used, so your sink might be one color while the countertop is another.

Location

No matter which sink you eventually decide on, it must be properly located within the kitchen to offer maximum function, for it forms the core of the food-preparation area and is one of the three components of the work triangle. (The range and refrigerator are the other two.)

According to the NKBA's kitchen design guidelines, plan at least 24 inches of countertop frontage to one side of the primary sink and 18 inches on the other side. This includes sinks installed in corners. The 24-inch length of counter frontage must be at the same height as the sink. (Measure countertop frontage only, do not count corner space.) The minimum allowable space from a corner to the edge of the primary sink is 3 inches.

Let There Be (Plenty of) Light

Millions of us grew up setting the table, drying the dishes and/or eating dinner in a kitchen that was illuminated by a single circular fluorescent fixture that cast a ghostly blue-green glow. But advances in lighting technology and design mean there's no need to squint your way through meal preparations and cleanup just because that's the way your grandmother or your mom did it.

The planning phase is also the time to be sure your new kitchen includes adequate lighting (both natural and artificial). Good lighting ensures that you'll not only be able to find your way into and around the kitchen but that you'll be able to perform cooking and cleanup tasks with ease. Be aware that the type and location of the lighting fixtures you select also affect the appearance and color of skin tones, wood species and fabrics, as well as the foods you prepare and serve in your kitchen.

Plan the amount and location of lighting fixtures carefully because changing them later is costly (the electrician and the spackling and painting crews), not to mention messy (cutting and patching the walls and ceiling). Keep in mind that the light emitted by a fixture depends not only on the type of bulb used in it but on the style of the fixture and on its placement. For example, a chandelier that uses incandescent bulbs generally gives off a warm light that shines in all directions. On the other hand, a recessed light can direct its beam of light downward in a cone shape. If you skimp and include too few of these, there will be dark pockets between the cones of light.

Selecting lighting has become a science unto itself. Here again a qualified kitchen designer can help. Or, if your kitchen design is especially complex, involving adjoining living spaces or high ceilings, for example, or if you simply want to create drama with a variety of lighting types, you might do best to consult with a professional lighting designer. (See Resources, page 144.) Another source of lighting design assistance is a knowledgeable salesperson where you purchase the lighting fixtures.

No matter who plans the lighting, every up-to-date kitchen should include a combination of two or more lighting types, namely incandescent, fluorescent and halogen fixtures. Each type has its advantages and disadvantages.

Incandescent lighting is the familiar lightbulb you've probably always used. Incandescent bulbs provide a warm, golden light that shows off skin and wood tones to their best advantage. While the resultant light is soft and warm, it can create shadows that make performing common kitchen tasks, such as chopping and slicing vegetables, difficult, if not downright hazardous. Incandescent light is best used for ambient or general lighting such as the chandelier mentioned above.

It's likely that the word *fluorescent* takes you back to that familiar blue-green glow of the kitchen you grew up in. But fluorescent bulbs and fixtures have come a long way in the last ten years. The newest generation of energy-efficient flourescents is available in a variety of sizes and shapes and in color-corrected tubes that more nearly approach the look of natural daylight. But you'll need to specify warm color-corrected bulbs. And be prepared to spend as much as $30 per bulb. Yes, the price is steep. But the new generation of fluorescent bulbs are engineered to last up to ten times longer than their predecessors and to use less energy in the process. Manufacturers are not shy about making the claim that these bulbs can actually recoup their initial cost in savings over their lifetime.

Halogen bulbs (another form of incandescent light) provide the cleanest, brightest, whitest light available. Be aware that since the halogen gas in the bulbs burns brighter and hotter, these bulbs give off more heat than other forms of incandescent lighting or than bulbs from the fluorescent family. If you are contemplating lighting your new kitchen with halogen fixtures, visit a lighting showroom where you can test the heat output of the models you are considering. While you are there, ask to turn the fixtures off and then listen. Some people find the slight "pinging" sound that some halogens make as they initially begin to cool down annoying.

Mix these three types of lighting to provide ambient, task and mood lighting. **Ambient or general light** is the light that fills a space so you can find your way into the room and then locate the faucet on the sink and the controls on the range. It's the light that enables you to locate the edge of the countertop, to find the cookbook you want and to search for the right utensil in the drawer.

Even if you include adequate ambient light, perhaps from a number of ceiling fixtures strategically located throughout the space, you'll still be slicing tomatoes and peeling vegetables in your own shadow unless you install adequate **task lighting.** That's the light that enables you to read the recipe you were searching for in that cookbook and to slice those tomatoes and not your fingers. Task lighting lets you know if you got the lipstick off the wine glass, if the chicken is cooked all the way through and if that *is* indeed mold you see on the cheese.

To ensure good task lighting, plan to install fixtures specifically designed to shine on each work center, for example, in the ceiling or soffit above the sink, in the range hood or under the wall cabinets above the range and underneath the wall cabinets in the food-preparation area. You'll find small diameter fluorescents and low-voltage halogen strip lights that are specifically designed for under-the-cabinet installation. A word of caution: Be careful that once these lights are installed you will not be looking into the glare of the bulb when you are seated at the snack bar or dining area across the room.

Finally, consider ways to illuminate the kitchen for dining, when you're entertaining or after you've left the room to work or to relax in an adjacent family room or dining area. Providing **mood lighting** can be as simple as requesting one or more dimmer switches (rheostats). Or, if plans call for displaying a collection in your new kitchen, consider installing low-voltage halogen fixtures inside a glass-fronted cabinet to highlight a collection while softly lighting the space. Tiny bulbs in the toekick or in an open soffit area can also provide soft mood lighting.

Let the Sun Shine In

Next, assess the natural light that enters the space. Even those who spend limited time in the kitchen should remember that weekend breakfasts and summertime suppers are generally all prepared by natural light. So if your present kitchen is dark and dreary at any time of the day, consider increasing the available natural light. Perhaps you have space for an additional or larger window? Would it be possible to open up a wall and add a sliding glass door? Or, if wall space is at a premium, consider a skylight if the structure of your home permits. One hint: Transom and clerestory windows, which are installed high on a wall, admit more light per square foot than do windows placed at standard height.

Whatever the source of the natural light in your kitchen, NKBA design guidelines recommend that the *minimum* window/skylight area should be at least 10% of the total square footage of the room. Therefore, if the space measures 300 square feet, the window area should total *at least* 30 square feet.

Finally, magnify the effect of both natural and artificial light by including light-colored surfaces, such as on the ceiling, countertops and flooring. Keep in mind that the colors you choose to decorate the space will affect the light throughout the new kitchen. Darker colors tend to absorb the light.

Ventilation

The energy crunch of the 1970s had a positive effect on the fuel efficiency, not to mention the comfort level, of the average American home. For the crunch prompted both existing home owners and new-home builders to do all they could to tighten up their castles against the onslaught of the elements. Insulation added to walls and attics and new or replacement energy-efficient windows and doors make today's homes more airtight than ever before.

Airtight homes are ideal from the standpoint of conserving energy resources, cutting heating and air-conditioning bills, and maintaining the physical comfort of the occupants. But airtight houses present a whole new set of problems: While the heat of summer and the cold of winter can't get into an airtight house, the moisture, smoke, heat and odors generated by cooking can't get out either. And it's not just a question of getting rid of the aroma of last night's garlic mashed potatoes or the family's favorite stuffed cabbage. Trapped moisture generated by cooking can do real harm by soaking insulation, rendering it forever useless, and by rotting the unseen structural members of a house. Unless you remove the heat generated by the range, your air-conditioning system will be working for naught the entire time you are cooking. And cooking grease that's not collected and removed becomes a fire hazard in the area near the range, and can and will coat every surface from cabinets and walls in the kitchen itself to furniture, windows and window treatments in adjoining rooms, in a matter of just a few months. All of which makes it more important than ever to include proper ventilation equipment in your new kitchen.

One Size Does Not Fit All

All ventilation systems are measured by the CFM (cubic feet per minute) of air they move. The higher the cfm rating, the more effective the air-flow rate and the more successfully the contaminants are captured and removed. NKBA guidelines call for a minimum rating *no less* than 150 cfm over a regular cooktop or range, and more for a grill/griddle-type range, which generates more smoke and heat.

Unless you have absolutely no other alternative, always select ventilation equipment that is ducted to the outside of the house. Recirculating fans are useless for removing steam, odors, smoke and grease.

There are two basic types of ventilation to consider, updraft and downdraft. Which you select will depend on the type of cooking appliance you choose, which in turn ought to hinge on the type of cooking (stir-frying, roasting, steaming) you do.

Freestanding or drop-in gas and electric ranges can be adequately vented by means of an exterior ducted updraft ventilation unit. These feature either a propeller-type fan or a squirrel cage wheel blower, located in a hood or canopy that's installed directly over the cooking surface. The hood acts as a trap for the heat and steam while the fan or blower removes them. For truly effective ventilation, the overhead range hood must be larger side to side and front to back than the cooktop or range it serves. Select a model that measures 6″ wider and is an inch or two deeper than the range you choose. The hood must also be tall enough to capture and hold the cooking vapor until the system can catch and vent it. And it's a must to follow the manufacturer's instructions in regard to the proper distance above the cooking surface to install the ventilation unit. Do not install a hood more than 30 inches above the cooking surface, according to NKBA guidelines.

Downdraft ventilation units are located at the same level as the cooking surface, or raised just slightly above. The ventilation on a downdraft unit works best when grilling, frying or using low pans because much of the steam that emanates from a tall pasta pot escapes a downdraft system, according to a 1989 engineering study conducted by the University of Minnesota. Another reason to carefully consider your preferred food preparation methods when choosing cooking and ventilation equipment: Downdraft units in islands or on peninsulas are subjected to cross air currents and are more difficult to vent properly, according to the same study. Island-based downdraft systems must be sized appropriately at a minimum of 250 cfm on up, depending on the number of burners and the size of the cooktop.

The effectiveness of any type of ventilation system is compromised by too long a run of the ducts. And ductwork that's the wrong size or with many elbows or turns results in a decrease in effectiveness as well. If you eventually evolve two acceptable floor plans for your new kitchen space and one provides a shorter duct run, keep this fact in mind.

No matter what type of unit you select, in order to be effective, ventilation equipment requires periodic maintenance. For most updraft units that's as simple as removing a wire-mesh filter and soaking it in the sink with a degreaser or perhaps running it through the dishwasher. Cleaning frequency depends on your preferred method of cooking. (Steaming and broiling generate fewer airborne grease particles than deep- or stir-frying.) Downdraft units, where grease is collected in a separate container below the cooktop, require more frequent and more immediate cleaning.

Finally, realize that many people don't use the ventilation system they have because of the noise it generates. If this is an issue in your home (those who have a hearing loss or who wear a hearing aid will be particularly sensitive), look for a unit with a low sones rating (a measure of noise output), particularly when the unit is set at the high speed. It may cost a few dollars more, but if it means the system will be used, and thus that you may avoid potential damage to your home, it's worth it. Another possibility: Consider a ventilation unit with a motor that can be installed at a remote location, such as the basement or utility room, to cut down on the noise.

It's easy to see how a few more minutes spent now, planning the smallest details, might well net more convenience each day over the lifespan of your new kitchen.

CHAPTER 8

Cabinets and Storage Details

*(A Place for Everything and
Everything in Its Place)*

Here's the part you've been waiting patiently for. Or perhaps the chapter you turned to first. It's not surprising that anyone who's thinking "new kitchen" begins with thinking "new cabinets," for the cabinetry is the single most important feature of your new kitchen. Not only does it provide the storage necessary to make the room function properly, it sets the overall decorative tone too. And it will most likely require the largest slice of your kitchen remodeling budget, representing anywhere from about one-third to one-half of the cost of your new kitchen. If you're planning a kitchen carrying an average price tag, say in the $18,000–$21,000 range, that means you'll be spending $6,000–$7,000 on cabinetry alone, even more if your budget is higher or you opt for a specialized custom cabinet. Reason enough to learn all you can about cabinets before you buy.

Stock Cabinets

No matter if you have your heart set on warm wood or sleek contemporary laminate, you'll first need to decide if you will purchase from either a stock or a custom line.

In the case of cabinetry, "stock" refers to standardized boxes that are manufactured in 3-inch-wide increments, starting with a 9-inch-wide tray cabinet on up to units as wide as 48 inches. Which means if the length of the kitchen walls is not evenly divisible by 3, there will be space left over at the end of the run or you'll need to use what's known as "fillers," narrow strips that match the cabinet finish and conceal gaps. All wall cabinets in a stock line measure a standard 12 inches deep and all base cabinets measure 24 inches deep.

Stock cabinets are available in a wide range of materials, finishes and door styles. Because the manufacturer can more closely control inventories of raw materials and keep a tight rein on production costs and schedules, stock cabinets are generally considerably less expensive than custom-manufactured cabinets. That does not mean that stock cabinets are necessarily always of lower quality than custom, particularly if you select from the middle to higher end of the stock manufacturer's price spectrum. And stock does not always mean that the cabinets are sitting in your dealer's warehouse waiting for immediate delivery. Most stock cabinet orders are assembled from pre-cut components and generally shipped within a few weeks time.

Of Note: Decorative moldings, applied in just the right places (to trim soffits, doorways and windows), add a finished, customized look to stock cabinets. Ask your cabinetmaker or kitchen and bath design professional for ideas on how you might further personalize a kitchen based on stock cabinetry with moldings, decorative hardware and/or interior fittings.

Custom Cabinets

Just as a custom-made suit or dress is cut and constructed to fit your exact measurements in fabrics and colors you select, custom-made cabinetry is produced on a job-by-job basis to fit the specific measurements of your room, in a style and color you choose. If you opt for custom-made units for your new kitchen, every inch of available space is occupied by a suitable cabinet. Custom units can be had in just about any wood variety or color, in any door style or design. With custom cabinetry, the style, design and interior options are limited only by your wallet and your imagination. Construction methods, labor and material costs are at the middle to high end of the price spectrum. If you opt for custom cabinets, expect to wait your turn in line behind previous orders anywhere from two to six months and to pay top dollar.

It's nearly impossible to tell the difference between stock and custom cabinets just by looking. So ask someone at your local kitchen and bath showroom to outline the crucial differences between his product offerings (many dealers carry a range) and then decide if they are important enough for you to pay the higher prices custom cabinets generally demand.

Look for a certification seal from the Kitchen Cabinet Manufacturers Association (see Resources, page 144). It tells you the manufacturer's products have been tested and meet some 60 of this trade association's requirements for construction and finish quality. However, not all manufacturers belong to the KCMA, and therefore some finer products, which may meet or even exceed standards, have not been tested.

Frame vs. Frameless

There was a time (prior to about 1983) when all American-made cabinetry was constructed with visible hinges and a face frame, or lip, around the inside of the cabinet box that could be seen when the doors were opened.

In the early 1980s, European manufacturers introduced the frameless method of construction, a system developed in Germany after World War II. (Hence the other name for frameless cabinetry—"Eurostyle." The terms "frameless" and "Eurostyle" are interchangeable.) The frameless method eliminates the face frame, gives access to the entire interior, allows hinges to be concealed and allows the doors to cover the entire opening of the cabinet box.

All things being equal, such as the quality of the raw materials, the drawer slides, the hardware, etc., cabinets constructed using the frameless method are equal in durability to frame units. So, as with so many other

components of your new kitchen, choosing between frame or frameless cabinets is strictly a matter of personal preference. Frameless construction provides a sleek cabinet interior with no frame inside the door to obstruct the view of, or access to, the interior. Some installers find frameless cabinetry a bit more time-consuming to install, which could be reflected in labor charges.

Cabinet Style

Most buyers are equally, if not more, concerned with a cabinet's styling as with its function. Here again, there are several options to choose from.

Wood and Wood Veneer

About 82% of the cabinets installed in kitchens were wood, according to the 1994 National Kitchen & Bath Association Trends Survey. Keep in mind that few, if any, of the wood cabinets you will see on your shopping forays are solid wood. Only top-of-the-line manufacturers offer solid wood doors, Because of cost, most wood cabinets produced today are made of plywood or one of several types of composite board substrate boxes, covered in a wood veneer and/or outfitted with solid wood doors. While higher in cost, the solid wood doors offer the advantage that they can be refinished if and when they start to show wear or if you tire of them and want a new look. Veneers, on the other hand, are usually less expensive but might allow you to use more exotic woods, such as bird's-eye maple, walnut, mahogany or rift-cut ash, that would otherwise be prohibitively costly. More and more manufacturers are using veneer because the doors are dimensionally more stable. (They warp and shrink less than solid wood.) And veneer presents a considerable savings to the environment.

It is the nature of wood to respond to humidity; thus, wood cabinetry may warp or shrink over time. Expect wood stains to darken and the grain to vary somewhat from door to door. And if you select a white painted wood cabinet, be aware that over time the expansion and contraction of the wood will cause dark lines to appear where pieces join. If you opt for wood cabinets, ask if the door is made of the same wood or the same veneer as the face frame, if there is one. All wood ages at different rates. So if you choose a cherry door on a maple face frame, the woods could darken at different rates. There's no need to pay for the entire box to be made out of solid cherry, but all the parts that show, such as the face frames and the side panels, should be constructed of the same wood variety. If the subtle gradations of grains and finish look like flaws to your eye, wood cabinets may not be for you.

If you're thinking of buying wood cabinets, the finish is the most important consideration for durability and long life. Whatever wood variety and finish you choose, examine cabinets carefully. The finish should look and feel perfectly smooth, with no bubbles, blisters, peeling or fine cracks, called crazing. And whether you choose a stain or paint look, your cabinets will most likely be finished with one of three major types of sealers.

The wide majority of today's wood cabinetry features a **catalyzed conversion varnish** finish that's applied over the stain color you choose. It's more expensive than other types of varnishes available because the curing or baking requires extra time. It's applied at the factory in a temperature-controlled and dust-free environment. The finish is resistant to moisture and skin oils and impervious to common household chemicals such as window cleaners, ammonia, vinegar, nail polish remover, wine and lemon juice, and wipes clean with a damp sponge.

Polyester finishes, generally applied over MDF (medium density fiberboard, a material made of fine wood fibers bonded with resins that offers superior screw holding power and cuts to a clean edge) substrates, offer a distinctive, dramatic, sophisticated, generally high-gloss look. Polyester cabinets are high-priced because the finishing process, which requires the application of many layers of meticulously applied clear or pigmented liquid polyester, is labor-intensive.

The higher the gloss on polyester, the more maintenance is required.

Polyester finishes can chip and are difficult, at best, to retouch or repair, but they are tougher than lacquer and are easily maintained with water and a soft cloth.

Lacquer finishes are easier, and thus cheaper, for manufacturers to apply. But they do tend to break down or yellow sooner than varnish, and they chip or nick easily and therefore are less durable. Lacquer is either a clear or pigmented liquid finish applied over stained or painted veneer or MDF door. It, too, is offered in a variety of sheens. A lacquer finish can chip or scratch, and is not as colorfast as catalyzed conversion varnish, polyester or thermofoil, but it can be retouched or repaired.

Laminates

If you favor a high-tech contemporary look, live with children or just want a really durable finish, your best cabinet material choice may be a laminate. In fact, even if you have your heart set on wood, don't rule out laminate cabinets. Some of today's reproduction wood grains are so lifelike Mother Nature herself would be hard put to tell the difference, thanks to new photographic techniques used in the production of the paper layers of the laminate.

The term "laminate" refers to any one of several different kinds of materials that are applied to various substrates. The quality of laminate cabinetry, currently used in about 15% of kitchens according to the NKBA survey, is determined by the composition of the substrate box, as well as the type of laminate applied to it. Don't fall for the common misconception that laminate cabinets are necessarily cheaper and/or of a lesser quality than wood cabinets. Again, all things such as hardware and construction methods being equal, that's just not true.

The highest quality laminate cabinetry is made with a medium density fiberboard underlayment covered with laminate. Laminate types include high-pressure laminate (HPL), which offers the best all-around performance. HPL, produced from several layers of kraft paper glued and pressed together, is glued to an MDF or particleboard substrate.

Low-pressure laminates (LPL), also called melamine or low-pressure melamine, are melamine-impregnated papers or polyester materials fused to a substrate by heat and pressure. Low-pressure laminates are less expensive, but not as impact-resistant and therefore not as durable, as high-pressure laminates. LPL are frequently used inside cabinets for a clean finish. (Be aware that all white or light-colored HPL or LPL laminates show a dark line at the edges.)

If you are partial to the look of painted cabinets, but hesitate because of concerns about chipping and cracking, investigate thermofoil cabinets. The newest entry on the laminate market, thermofoil cabinets are not, as their name might imply, shiny silver. Thermofoil is a stiff sheet of rigid foil PVC with color and/or pattern added. The foil sheet is heated and pressed to conform to a substrate (of varying grades and types, depending on the manufacturer, but mostly MDF and particleboard). Thermofoil is generally more durable than low-pressure laminates, lacquers and some polyesters. Thermofoil products are significantly less costly to produce than most painted cabinets because the manufacturing process is one step, as opposed to as many as eighteen steps for some of the paintlike finishes. Pricewise, thermofoil technology fills the gap between MDF and veneer finishes and high-pressure laminate.

Thermofoils resist household chemicals and stains and are available in colors ranging from pure white to faux woods and granites. Because the color is trapped within the PVC, thermofoil cabinetry is especially resistant to fading and yellowing, a particularly important feature if you have your heart set on white. And there is no dark line at the edge like you might see on some laminates. On the downside, thermofoil doors can scratch and are difficult, if not downright impossible, to repair.

Vinyl is a film that's heat-laminated to the surface using adhesives. Its biggest advantage is its low cost, but it is less durable and offered in limited designs and colors. Vinyl is generally best reserved for use on the inside of cabinets, which are subject to less wear, tear and scrubbing than exterior surfaces.

No matter which laminate you select, be aware that the various components used in their production exude fumes and gases for several months after their initial production, which could influence your decision if family members suffer from allergies. All laminates are easily maintained by wiping with a damp sponge or cloth, but be sure to check individual manufacturer's specifications for details.

The Hallmarks of Cabinet Quality

What does make a difference in the quality and price of cabinets? How do you choose good-quality cabinetry that will stand up to all the wear and tear, and yes, the abuse, that the average family is capable of dishing out? Any number of factors contribute to the quality, and thus dictate the price, of a cabinet line. But don't use price as your only criterion. And don't just look at the outside. When you shop for new cabinetry, look for the following hallmarks of a quality product:

Are the shelf positions adjustable? While you won't move the shelves often, having the capability to do so offers more storage flexibility over the life of your kitchen. Over the 20-year lifespan of the average kitchen it's entirely possible to go from storing tiny jars of baby food to finding space for dozens of large economy-sized boxes of cereal. And be sure to ask about the thickness of the shelves. Shelving that's $1/2$ inch thick is adequate to span lengths less than 36 inches, but $3/4$-inch-thick shelving is required so it won't bow over time if the shelf will span a larger space.

The finish on the inside of the cabinets is important too. Less expensive units feature unfinished particleboard interiors, which may be difficult to keep clean. The next rung up on the quality ladder is a vinyl interior, followed by natural wood veneer. Next on the quality ladder you'll find a melamine interior (a low-pressure laminate) that's usually available in a choice of white or almond, followed in cost and durability by the top-of-the-line high-pressure laminate interior.

Functional hardware, such as the drawer slides and door hinges, tell a great deal about the quality of the cabinets. Hardware with all metal (as opposed to plastic) working parts, which can be expected to stand up to 15 or 20 years of daily wear and tear, is a sign of good quality.

Drawer glides or slides should attach to both sides, or run under the drawer, so they'll operate smoothly and evenly over the life of the kitchen. Check to see if the glides allow the drawer to extend fully so you don't have to rummage about in dark, back corners for the paring knife, a book of matches, or the egg slicer. Be sure that they lock in place at the end of the run so you can't inadvertently pull the drawer, and its contents, all the way out. And look for a minimum load rating of about 50 pounds. The highest-quality glides are able to carry a load of 150 pounds, which means if your kids decide to use the open drawers as a handy ladder to reach the cookie jar, the cookies may not survive but the drawer, and your kids, will.

Pull out a drawer and check to see how it's assembled. Drawers that are simply glued at the corners do not hold up as well as those constructed with a combination of glue and nails or glue and staples. Top-quality drawers are made with dowels or dovetailed or dadoed (where one component slides into a grooved slot on the other). For easy cleaning, look for drawer interiors lined with melamine, laminate or vinyl and not simply a raw piece of particleboard.

Planning With Storage in Mind

If you're tired of tripping over the trash can, rummaging on your hands and knees for that pot lid, untangling yards of small appliance cords or keeping the dog food in the laundry room, now is the time to plan to eliminate those snags with your new kitchen plan. If inadequate storage is one of your top reasons for considering a kitchen makeover, there are several steps you can take during the planning process to ensure that your new kitchen functions optimally and looks great.

How many cabinets will you need? The answer depends on exactly what you plan to store in your new kitchen. Rather than trying to fit your possessions into your new spaces, build or customize the storage to suit what you own. The first step in planning your new storage is to clean out the old. Discard all the gadgets and gizmos you have not used in the last year or so. Then take stock of what you own. Don't forget the food processor, mixer or fish poacher you plan to purchase for your new kitchen, or to allow for future expansion of your cooking and serving pieces later on. Take stock of what you would like to be able to store in your new kitchen that doesn't fit now. This might include cleaning items such as a broom and dustpan, mop, and vacuum or your ironing board and iron. Measure odd-shaped items (such as that collector's pitcher, the holiday turkey platter, your antique chafing dish, trays, extra tall wine glasses, etc.) and plan accordingly. Drawers that pull out to bring the contents of the cabinet forward to you offer the best accessibility, require less movement and eliminate stooping. Plan what suits your needs best. Your goal is to optimize the potential of every cabinet and every inch of space. Racks, bins, dividers, hooks and pullouts can all contribute to improved storage capabilities. But at $50–$100 per unit, they can also add considerably to the final remodeling tally. So analyze your storage needs carefully before you choose. And select only those that suit your life and cooking style. Look for lazy Susans, corner lazy Susans, flip-down sink-front units to store sponges, rubber gloves, etc. Install a narrow, pullout drying rack to keep wet dish towels out of sight. Consider a spice drawer or rack, built-in cutting boards, a wine rack, pigeonhole drawers, display shelves, a built-in ironing board, mixer or food-processor stand. Or opt for vertical dividers in a narrow (say 15-inch-wide) base cabinet to keep the lids and cookie sheets neatly organized and handy. Use the wasted area above a standard-height refrigerator to stash trays and platters on several shallow shelves. Here are some additional storage tips:

- **Look up and down.** To solve your storage needs, explore the possibility of eliminating the soffit (the wallboard box that usually extends from the top of the cabinets to the ceiling) and installing 42-inch-tall, as opposed to 30-inch-tall, wall cabinets. While you won't want to store frequently used items on those shelves above your head, it's the ideal location for stashing infrequently used items. Don't forget to include storage for a small stepladder in your plan.

Many cabinet manufacturers now provide a variety of storage options that make efficient use of previously wasted toekick space. Choose a built-in stepladder, or a shallow drawer to stash pot lids, cookie trays or the newspaper and cardboard awaiting recycling. Look for a unit with a specialized holder that allows you to slide pet food dishes out from underfoot.

- **Consider a countertop appliance garage.** With a rollup tambour door, an appliance garage (or even two) provides an efficient and convenient way to make use of previously wasted countertop corners. It provides a spot to keep those small appliances such as the toaster, coffee grinder and maker you use frequently within easy reach but out of sight the remainder of the time. And not only does a centralized small appliance storage location cut down on countertop clutter and on the number of steps it takes to prepare a meal, it also frees up precious shelf space inside the cabinets to store other items. Be sure to include at least one electrical outlet either inside the garage or nearby.

- **Plan a pantry.** Nowadays it's the rare kitchen that boasts enough space to accommodate a walk-in pantry like the one Grandma's country kitchen offered. And while most of us no longer require an entire enormous pantry room to store the bounty of summer's harvest for the next three seasons, a pantry cabinet does make it possible to stock up on frequently used items, take advantage of sales or promotions, or simply cut down on the number of necessary trips to the supermarket.

Most manufacturers now supply a wide variety of cabinet shapes and sizes designed to act as pantry storage. Options include shallow units to recess between the studs or at the end of a run of cabinets; tall, columnar pullout units to flank the refrigerator; wire-coated baskets and bins that pull out on heavy-duty rollers to transform a tall 15-to-18-inch-wide unit into a spacious pantry. Don't be tempted to design a pantry any deeper than 18 inches. The resultant "extra" 6 inches are all but inaccessible.

• **Hide the trash.** Simply by concealing the trash bin on a rollout under the sink or in a base cabinet adjacent to the dishwasher, it is possible to remove a major eyesore and common stumbling block from the kitchen. Or take the idea one step further and include a recycling center in your plans for a new kitchen. (See Chapter 5, Environmental Concerns, page 45.) Include divided bins for glass, plastics and compostable items under the sink or in the pantry. Manufacturers now offer recycling units in a variety of sizes, shapes, materials and configurations. Your selection should be based on the space you have available and on your particular recycling needs.

• **Include a planning desk.** Ideally, every home could use a spot where family members can file favorite recipes, stash cookbooks, write the shopping list, store coupons and plan meals, parties and holiday menus. The kitchen is also an ideal place for keeping track of family activities, school events, and children's calendars. If space allows, set aside a corner of your new kitchen to use as a mission control center for your home. Include file drawers to organize appliance warranty information, repair-service telephone numbers and other necessary household information. Plan open shelves to store your favorite cookbooks close at hand. And the kitchen desk is the logical location for a telephone, pens, pencils, a message pad and the local telephone directory. If it is possible to incorporate a planning desk into your kitchen, you will find it is one of the most used areas in your home.

There are more than 200 nationally distributed manufacturers in the U.S.

who produce cabinets in a wide spectrum of price and quality. And you'll also find innumerable small, local cabinet shops, or regionally distributed manufacturers who likewise offer a wide range of products. It isn't necessary to purchase from a nationally distributed manufacturer to get good looks and a quality product. But if you do decide to work with a less well-known regional manufacturer, or with a local custom shop, be sure to get several references and then follow up. Call the references or, better yet, pay a personal visit to a local custom manufacturer's client or two.

It should be clear by now that price shouldn't be your only determinant when selecting cabinetry. Budget considerations, the overall value of your home, and the length of time you intend to stay there should all be factored into your decision to buy at the low, medium or high end of the field. No matter what your decision, there are any number of cabinets out there to choose from so that you end up with a kitchen that suits your style and boasts a place for everything.

Of Note: Here are several rules of thumb to help you plan efficient storage.

- *Group like items together, at the point of first or last use; for example, dishes near the dishwasher or the eating area.*

- *Plan a spot for every item at the work center where you will use it; for example, measuring spoons near the cooktop, and/or in the food preparation area, cleaning supplies near the sink. It may be necessary to duplicate some items in a two-cook kitchen.*

- *Aim for clear visibility of all supplies. Avoid nesting and stacking items one on top of another.*

- *For safety's sake, plan to keep heavy or bulky items, such as the pasta pot and food processor, nearer to the floor than to the ceiling.*

CHAPTER 9

Major Appliances

(Picking and Choosing the Big-Ticket Items)

In order to keep the cost of remodeling your kitchen in line with your budget, you may be considering saving a bit by reinstalling your old appliances in your new kitchen. Think again. In the last decade every major appliance manufacturer has made advances in energy efficiency and design, as well as added new convenience features across all product categories. Unless your existing appliances are less than a year or two old, replacing them with current models might just be your smartest move, for a number of reasons. Improved energy efficiency saves on the cost of running appliances, in some cases so dramatically that it's possible to recoup all of your original investment over the lifetime of the appliance. Conve-

Of Note: According to AHAM (the Association of Home Appliance Manufacturers), improvements in energy efficiency translate into substantial savings on the cost of running an appliance over its life span. When comparing 1971 models with 1992 models, the cost of operating the average refrigerator for a year dropped from $142 to $71, a dishwasher from $110 to $71, a clothes washer from $131 to $92, and a freezer from $120 to $50.

nience features and time-savers, as well as safety features, add to your comfort. Streamlined styling and electronic touch-pad controls make it possible to clean up spatters and spills with one wipe.

How to Choose

There are several general rules of thumb to follow when choosing and placing appliances:

Know your needs and, once again, your lifestyle. As with every other product category, you'll find a wide price spectrum for appliances. Do your homework on which features are worth the money to you. The extra cost of a frost-free refrigerator and a self-cleaning oven spread out over an estimated dozen or more years of ownership might well be worth it in terms of the time and labor you'll save. Ditto the cost of a time-delay cycle on the dishwasher that allows you to take advantage of running the machine at off-peak hours and at reduced power rates, but only if that option is available from your local utility company. Fine china and pot washing cycles add to the cost of the dishwasher.

Your family may now consist of four or five members, but if your kids are off to college in a few years, that large freezer compartment may remain mostly empty. Or, it might just be the two of you now, but if you're planning additions to your family in the near future, choose a refrigerator, laundry equipment, dishwasher, etc. that will accommodate that anticipated growth. Those who entertain a great deal might consider not one, but two, dishwashers, a warming oven, a wine cooler and modular refrigeration units in their kitchen plans.

Remember that the appliances are the true workhorses of your kitchen. If at all possible, try not to economize by buying at the lower end of the price spectrum. Instead, select the best appliances you can afford. To keep an eye on the budget and for the lowest prices, look for special purchase units or model year-end clearance sales, which may mean the model you've chosen is discontinued. There's nothing wrong with purchasing a recently discontinued model as long as it meets your needs, though be aware that its features may not be the latest, and parts might be more difficult to obtain farther down the road.

Check and double-check measurements to be sure that all the models you are considering will fit through hallways and doors and into the kitchen space on installation day and that once in place, correct clearances allow all doors to open without blocking passages or interfering with cabinet functions. You do not want to create a situation in which the oven can't be opened at the same time as an adjacent drawer, for example. To aid in your decision, ask your appliance dealer for the specification sheets on the models you are considering. Use them to keep track of the measurements, capacities, features and designs.

Finally, no matter what the appliance, always check exactly what is covered by the warranty and for how long. And then factor that information into your decision. Be sure to put each appliance through its paces and to use each feature and each control or cycle, at least once, shortly after your new appliances are installed. In addition to familiarizing yourself with the new equipment, you are testing it. Most defects covered under the warranty will show up during the first few uses. But if, for example, the oven-cleaning feature is not used during the warranty period, repairs will probably not be covered by the time you discover the problem.

Dishwashers

The first dishwasher made its appearance on the American home scene about 1890. Use grew slowly, partly because home economists as well as the general public viewed the time spent loading, unloading and cleaning it as excessive. In the 1960s, the dishwasher began to lose its aura as a luxury item for an elite few when manufacturers were able to refine the machines and eliminate the need to prerinse, thereby saving water and time. And by 1994, kitchen designers who were members of the National Kitchen & Bath Association reported that 94% of the kitchens they installed in the prior year included at least one dishwasher.

When it comes to dishwashers today, advances in technology are measured in terms of "less," not "more." The most noticeable improvement in the dishwasher category over recent years has been the reduction of the noise the machines make while in operation. All major brands now include varying amounts and types of sound-deadening insulation, an especially important feature if the kitchen you're planning is open to the family room where other activities are taking place.

Because of recent Department of Energy standards that mandate the energy use of each cycle, newer dishwasher models require less water to function optimally. (Most of the energy required by a dishwasher is to heat the water; thus the less water used, the less energy consumed.) An effective dishwasher eliminates the need to rinse or prewash, and thus saves even more water. And for every gallon saved, there's a corresponding saving in the cost of heating the water. All of which translates into a lower energy cost to operate the unit over its lifetime.

Of Note: Most of today's American-made dishwashers operate on from 8 to about 11 gallons of water, depending on manufacturer and model; the generally higher-priced European models require even less. That's a dramatic savings over the 15.7 gallons a study conducted for the Association of Home Appliance Manufacturers (AHAM) found was required to wash the same number of dishes by hand.

Dishwasher effectiveness is influenced by the number (one, two or three) and location (top, bottom and center) of water sources. Washing action is also affected by the pattern of the water spray and the size and number of holes in the arm; the smaller the holes, the finer the spray, the greater the water pressure, and thus the more effective the washing action.

In addition to the amount and the pattern of the water spray, the water temperature is important to cleaning action too. So models that offer a built-in heater that either brings cold water to the optimal 140 degrees and/or maintains that temperature during operation cost more and work more effectively than a model with no heater. That temperature, by the way, is much too hot for safe showers and baths, particularly if you share your home with small children or older adults, so do not be tempted to set the house water heater any higher than 120 degrees.

A self-cleaning filtering system, usually a mesh screen that strains food particles and keeps them from redepositing on clean dishes, as well as an internal food disposer that chops food into particles small enough to drain off in the rinse water, add to the cost, as well as to the effectiveness, of many models.

Racks, too, differ in the materials they are coated with. Most are made of metal coated with vinyl (PVC). More expensive units feature a tougher nylon coating. A thicker layer of coating will last longer and not rub off to expose the metal underneath. Racking capabilities have been refined to include pull-down shelves for cups and glasses and shelves that can be adjusted to hold larger items, such as mixing bowls and cookie sheets. On top-of-the-line machines, the racks too should be covered under the warranty.

Other differences to consider include the length and type of drying cycle options and the number of wash cycles. A stainless-steel interior is more costly, but practically indestructible. Convenience features you might want to consider include delay start and a rinse dispenser.

On the exterior, recent model dishwashers (as well as the other appliances) feature clean, uncluttered styling. In addition to the standard interchangeable black and/or white panels for doors and toekick access panels that are shipped with most units, many dishwashers (and refrigerators and trash compactors too) are designed to accept decorative laminate, stainless steel or wood panels as long as the edges of the panels are no more than $1/4$ inch thick.

According to the NKBA kitchen design guidelines, the dishwasher should be within 36 inches of the edge of one sink. Ideally, it should be reachable by more than one person at a time so two cooks or helpers can work. Allow a minimum of 21 inches of clear floor space between the edge of the dishwasher and counters, other appliances and/or cabinets located at right angles to the dishwasher.

Refrigerators

Refrigerators are measured by the cubic foot and range from units as small as 2.5 cubic feet to nearly 30 cubic feet. Home economists have long recommended that a minimum of 8–10 cubic feet will serve two family members well. Add at least one more cubic foot per additional family member. But if you entertain a great deal, live on fresh vegetables or cook and freeze in batches, you might want to consider an even larger model.

There are many different styles and configurations of refrigerators, all designed to meet a variety of needs and lifestyles and satisfy a range of budget requirements. If aesthetics are a major concern for you, choose a sleek and unobtrusive built-in. Side-by-side refrigerator models offer two full-length compartments, one a freezer, the other a refrigerator. Caution: Be sure the types of foods your family enjoys can be conveniently stored in this configuration. Some frozen pizzas, for example, cannot lie flat on a shelf and some side-by-side units may not be wide enough for your largest platters and serving pieces. If you have a large family, or cook and freeze in batches, you might best be served by separate single-door freezer-only and refrigerator-only units.

Freezer-above-and-refrigerator-below models as well as refrigerator-above-and-freezer-below models offer proportionately more refrigerator space than do side-by-side models. And they can be dressed up with panels to match your cabinetry. Choose a model that offers the option of changing the hinges from one side to the other, or be sure to order the correct hinge location for your new kitchen layout. Consider a freezer-on-the-bottom unit if you would like to avoid bending and stooping. This design places most of the refrigerator storage between your eyes and your knees and relegates the less frequently used freezer storage to the bottom. Small modular units can do the same. Glass doors allow you a clear view of the content without opening the refrigerator, but clutter and food packages are also prominently displayed. Check to see that crisper drawer rollers glide smoothly. And double-check the manufacturer's specifications for height, width and depth as well as for the side-to-side clearance requirements for the model you are considering. It's obvious what will happen if the height or width of the refrigerator does not fit the space you have, but if the door doesn't have proper clearance, it won't open fully and you won't have complete access to the crisper bins. Are the drawers deep enough to suit your eating habits? Two crisper drawers provide flexibility for fruit and vegetable storage. What are the shelves made of? Solid shelves contain spills; wire shelves do not, which might be of major importance if it's the kids who rummage for the juice each morning. Adjustable split-width shelving provides more storage flexibility than full-width shelving. Be aware that it's entirely possible for two models with identical cubic-foot capacity to feature different total shelf area measurements. Check the manufacturer's specifications on all models you are considering, and compare the pros and cons of each.

The least glamorous parts of the refrigerator, such as the insulation, gaskets, door seals and compressor, all affect its daily performance. Adjustable wheels and locks, interior lighting, well-placed and easy-to-read controls, clear bins, slide-out shelves and specialized storage bins add convenience. An ice maker that provides cubes and/or crushed ice, freezer baskets, adjustable freezer shelves, a wine rack, etc., can add to the cost and are desirable options—but only if they suit your needs.

It is still possible to find refrigerators that must be defrosted manually by turning them off several times a year and removing the ice and water yourself. A partially automatic refrigerator requires manual defrosting of the freezer section. Automatic defrosting units keep the freezer frost-free at all times but may use more power to do so.

In recent years, the Department of Energy, the Environmental Protection Agency, public and private utility companies and major appliance manufacturers have all been hard at work engineering more energy-efficient and environmentally sound models of refrigerators. So for the first time in nearly 50 years, the latest generations of refrigerators are significantly different from previous models due to technological changes. These changes were fueled by two pieces of legislation: one that calls for eliminating chlorofluorocarbons (CFCs) from refrigerants, another that requires developing units that use less electricity. Several rounds of energy-use requirements mandated by the Department of Energy have already gone into effect, and yet another, unspecified round of energy use cutbacks is scheduled to be put into effect by January 1, 1998.

The passage of the Clean Air Act Amendment of 1990 allowed the Environmental Protection Agency to mandate that manufacturers of refrigeration appliances (refrigerators, freezers, dehumidifiers, home and automobile air conditioners) eliminate all chlorofluorocarbon refrigerants from their products by January 1, 1996. Currently, CFCs are found in two different components of all the refrigerators manufactured in recent decades: CFC 12 is the fluid in the refrigeration system, and CFC 11 is used to activate the blown-in foam insulation in the walls of the box.

Why are CFCs banned? Because they deplete the ozone layer. While the ban is a sound ecological move, it is somewhat at odds with the Department of Energy's agenda. The DOE goals require appliance manufacturers to improve the energy efficiency of all their products, a double whammy for refrigerator manufacturers because existing cooling technology, as well as alternative refrigerants, proved less effective than CFC refrigerants.

To offset shortfalls in refrigerator performance and at the same time reduce energy consumption, manufacturers have made modifications, such as redesigning compressors, blowers and refrigeration systems; increasing insulation; improving gaskets and sealing systems; altering the shape of the interior and the placement of insulation and developing smarter control systems. All of these small changes add up to large improvement.

But the best news for homeowners is a lower electric bill. The expected energy use on the most efficient refrigerator models currently available is estimated at $55 per year at the national average of 8.25 cents per kilowatt hour.

> *Of Note:* *The Department of Energy mandates began with refrigerators because, of all home appliances, they consume the most energy—as much as 12% to 20% of the total power used by the average household in one year, depending on the size and vintage of the model—primarily because they run 24 hours a day.*

So what does all this mean for the homeowner who's shopping for a re-frigerator? The twin challenge of energy efficiency and the elimination of all CFCs can be expected to drive product costs up, at least in the short run. The substitute materials for CFCs are more expensive and, because they are less efficient, there are more components involved. Traditionally, though, over the long haul, markets tend to strive for better value, which is certainly the case with other recent technological advances, such as the VCR, the video camera and the personal computers. And at any rate, the higher price, anticipated to be about $100 over the last generation's models, should be recouped via energy savings over the life of the refrigerator.

The new models will have almost the same cubic-foot capacity. The door will be 1¼ inch thicker than on earlier models, and they won't be any larger on the outside. There are simply too many existing kitchens with just the right amount of space for today's model sizes.

Not only will the next generation of refrigerators boast improved energy efficiency, but they've been redesigned on the inside, so they make more sense. Doors conveniently stash larger items, such as one-gallon milk and juice containers. On many models hinges can be switched, altering the di-rection in which the door swings and thus eliminating the concern when you order and enabling you to move the refrigerator to another kitchen with a different layout if necessary. Bins are installed on heavy-duty rollers so they can hold large packages and heavier items. Solid shelves prevent spills from spreading and, along with clear bins, make it easy to find what you're looking for. And it's now possible to find more models in more price ranges that will fit flush with cabinetry to simulate the popular built-in look.

Manufacturers continue to add new bells and whistles to refrigerators. But features such as capacity, storage flexibility, adequate interior lighting, spill-resistant shelving and options such as ice makers and wine racks are expected to remain the same. The most efficient models sport a sophisticated defrosting system that works only when it is needed and uses vacuum panel insulation technology in place of CFCs.

When locating the refrigerator within the kitchen, plan at least 15 inches of countertop space on the latch side of a single door model or on either side of a side-by-side unit. Another option: 15 inches of countertop space across from the refrigerator, but no more than 48 inches away. Though not ideal, it is acceptable to place an oven adjacent to a refrigerator, according to NKBA guidelines.

Cooking Equipment

The selection of cooking appliances depends on a number of factors, not the least of which is the type and quantity of foods you prepare. Those who entertain a great deal and who regard cooking as a favorite activity will choose appliances differently from those who don't know, or care to learn, the difference between sear and sauté, or a grill and a griddle.

Like everything else in your kitchen, the cost of cooking equipment will affect your selection. Cost in cooking equipment is influenced by the quality of the components, such as the hinges and racks, the type of timer and controls, as well as the door seals and indicator lights. Optional features, such as the ability to self-clean, a larger oven cavity, and a delay-start cooking control that allows the chicken to roast and the potatoes to brown while you run the babysitter home and pick up the dry cleaning, will also add to the cost.

Another top concern when choosing cooking gear is the ease with which

it cleans up. Your dollars might be well spent on models that offer smooth control panels, glass-top surfaces, sealed burners, self-cleaning ovens, lift-up tops, and removable control knobs that get the cleanup crew out of the kitchen and on to other activities sooner.

And unless you're a professional cooking instructor, caterer or gourmet chef, appliance appearance is probably not tops on your list of demands. In fact, most cooks don't want the appliances to stand out, just work hard and live long.

Provided you have access to both types of fuel, you'll need to choose between gas or electric appliances or a combination of both. Among professional chefs and serious cooks, there is no contest: Gas burners offer instantaneous response and minute control, while electric ovens are preferred for their even heat.

Whether you're wedded to gas or electric cooking appliances or to a combination of both, the next step to narrowing your selections is to choose between a freestanding range that offer burners and an oven in one unit, or separate and independently installed cooktop and oven(s).

Freestanding gas or electric ranges are designed for installation between cabinets or on the end of a run of cabinets. The most common size is 30 inches wide, and it is possible to find both 24-inch and 36-inch widths. All feature a built-up back panel that displays a clock, timer, light and other accessories. Drop-in models sit on a low cabinet base or hang from a countertop. Slide-in range units rest on the floor, have no back panel and provide somewhat of a built-in look.

Separate gas or electric cooktops are most commonly available in 30-inch and 36-inch widths. The narrower units offer four burners or elements, while the wider units may offer five or even six. Cooktops are generally paired with one, or sometimes two, wall ovens in 24-inch, 27-inch or 30-inch widths. (An oven cavity size of about 4 cubic feet is considered adequate for most cooks' needs.) Because they can be located independently, this option is a wise choice for a kitchen where two cooks will be working at the same time and it's desirable to separate the functions. A separate wall oven can be installed under the counter (be sure to check specifications and verify that the model is UL approved for such an installation), at waist height or at eye level, according to individual need. Separate units lend a sleek, built-in, contemporary look for those whose top concern is aesthetics.

Thermal convection cooking, used by the pros for years, was until the last year or two available only in separate electric wall oven models but can now even be found in some freestanding gas and electric range models. Thermal convection is most appreciated by those who bake or prepare large amounts of food. Convection units include a separate heat source and fan, mounted on an oven wall. When the oven is switched to the convection mode, hot air is blown into the oven cavity to completely surround the food. Not only does food cook more evenly and retain more moisture, but baking takes less time.

Whether you choose gas or electric, you'll need to make a choice between oven cleaning modes. At the lower end of the price spectrum it's still possible to find basic range models that require manual cleaning. Look for a unit with removable oven doors and lift-up bake elements to make this chore easier. Self-clean (pyrolitic) ovens feature a separate, several-hour-long cycle during which the oven temperature can reach up to 900 degrees. The intensity and duration of this heat reduces spills and grease to a powder that can easily be wiped up with a damp cloth. Continuous-clean ovens are made with a rough, porous interior surface designed to resist stains and partially absorb grease. For ideal function, racks must be removed from all types of ovens and manually cleaned. If you favor a spotlessly clean oven, continuous-clean may not be for you.

Gas cooking equipment offers instant response and easy heat control, and accommodates a wide range of pan sizes and materials. In recent years, gas cooktop manufacturers have developed sealed burners so boilovers can't get down into the body of the range or extinguish the flame. Sealed burners are slightly more expensive than standard burner ranges in which the burners are removable and the top lifts up for cleaning. Look for a model with pilotless ignition, which saves energy, over models with a pilot light that burns constantly.

Electric ranges and cooktops are often attractive to families that include small children, because there is no open flame. And top-of-the-range cooking with electricity is somewhat cooler than with gas.

The familiar coiled elements are the least expensive electric alternative. The coiled elements heat up quickly and accommodate a variety of cookware but perform best when the pot and the coil are close to each other in size. Drip pans below the coils catch spills and boilovers.

Solid elements are cast-iron disks sealed into the cooking surface so spills can not seep under into the burner box. Sleek and contemporary solid elements, sometimes called hobs, require the use of heavy-gauge, flat-bottom metal pots and pans to maintain good contact with the heat source. Cookware should be sized to the elements, so if your cooking needs call for large batches in oversize fry pans, canners, etc., that even the largest solid elements don't match up with, you may be better off selecting a model with coil elements or a gas unit. Solid elements are generally somewhat slower to respond than standard elements. So if you're the impatient type and you still want solid elements, look for disks that offer thermostatic controls to maintain a preset temperature, of course, at a higher cost.

Ceramic glass cooktops feature electric elements (though gas ceramic glass tops are in development stages at this writing) sealed under a durable, smooth, easy-to-clean, generally black, glass ceramic top. This generation of ceramic glass is more durable and stain-resistant than previous generations of white glass ceramic tops, though they can scratch and do stain with certain foods. Again, heavy-gauge, flat-bottom cookware works best. Cookware may extend no more than two inches beyond the cooking area. Because the heat source is farther removed from the food, cooking on ceramic glass tops can take a few minutes longer. And ceramic glass cooktops take some time to cool after use—a possible disadvantage, again, if you live with small children—but most feature an "on" indicator light. Some ceramic glass top manufacturers recommend cleaning with a special cleaner or with baking soda and water.

Of Note: Every ceramic glass top you will find is made from glass supplied by just one manufacturer, Schott, and sold under the brand name Ceran™.

Often one or two halogen elements are included on some electric ceramic glass cooktops. These units feature glass tubes filled with the same halogen gas used for bright, white halogen lighting, sealed under a ceramic glass top. Halogen elements glow instantly when turned on and reach higher temperatures than standard electric elements but do cost more.

Induction cooking equipment is the most expensive, but also the most responsive, and easily controlled, of the electric offerings. This system works via an induction coil sealed under the glass ceramic surface. Electric current flows through the coil and creates a magnetic field, therefore you must use a magnetic pan (common magnetic materials in most kitchens include cast iron, steel and enamel on steel). The molecules in the pan are set into motion, which generates heat that transfers only to the pot and to the food, not to the cooktop, so spills don't cook on and the cooktop itself remains cool.

Both gas and electric equipment manufacturers offer grill cooktop or range models that allow you to enjoy the flavor of grilled foods indoors all year round. These units offer the versatility of interchangeable, modular accessories including a griddle, rotisserie, wok, or deep fryer and the added flexibility of mixing gas and electric modules in one unit. However, with this type of cooking, smoke, grease and odors must be vented *to the outside* via a high-powered exhaust system and ductwork that's installed either overhead or under the cooktop (downdrafted). Even the quietest of these units generates quite a bit of noise, which could be a factor in selection for some. Avoid creating a vent run that's too long, or with many elbows, that could render the exhaust system ineffective. And if you opt for separate, overhead ventilation, consult with a kitchen design professional or carefully follow the manufacturer's specifications for correct sizing and placement. (See Chapter 7, Your Kitchen Sink, page 67.) On the downside, grill units require immediate, heavy-duty cleanup.

In an open plan configuration, allow at least 9 inches of countertop space on one side of a cooktop or range and at least 15 inches on the other. Allow at least 3 inches of clearance space from an end wall that's protected by flame-retardant surfacing materials and provide a minimum of 15 inches of countertop on the other side. The countertops on either side of a range or cooktop must be at the same height as the appliances, according to the NKBA design guidelines. If the cooktop is located in an island, countertop must also extend behind the cooking surface and at the same height. The cooking surface should not be located under a window, unless the window is at least 3 inches behind the appliance and at least 24 inches above it. For safety's sake, the window should not be dressed with a flammable treatment.

You'll need to plan at least 15 inches of landing space adjacent to or above the oven if the appliance opens into a primary traffic aisle. If it doesn't open into the traffic pattern, you can plan the 15 inches of landing space across from the oven, but not more than 48 inches away, according to the NKBA design guidelines.

Commercial Lookalikes

Serious cooks are intrigued by professional restaurant or commercial-grade appliances for serious reasons: larger cooking, baking and storage capacities; the lightning-fast heat recovery on ranges and ovens and humidity control of refrigerators/freezers; the at-your-fingertips versatility offered by built-in griddles, grills and broilers; the durability of cast-iron, stainless-steel and baked-enamel surfaces and the ruggedness of welded steel construction.

And not-so-serious cooks are drawn to the same commercial appliances for reasons of their own: the high-tech look, visual impact and the status of owning a kitchen full of appliances whose combined price tags can effortlessly exceed $15,000. But a true commercial range cannot be used safely in any residential kitchen, a fact that local building supervisors, fire departments, the National Kitchen & Bath Association, the American Gas Association and any reputable kitchen designer will attest to. The chief reason: The high heat output, so effective for gourmet cooking, also presents a fire hazard. In fact, when all the burners are functioning at full tilt, commercial ranges give off more heat than most furnaces. This translates into the need for maintaining proper clearances from combustible surfaces, such as wallboard, wood structural components and cabinetry, as well as including tile or stainless-steel backsplashes and/or floor. In some building code jurisdictions, sprinklers must be installed. And because of the heat, ventilation equipment must be upgraded to keep pace with the range. In some cases commercial-grade cooking and refrigeration equipment weighs considerably more than residential counterparts, meaning that floor joists must be added to support the extra heft.

If you are still interested in either the look or the performance of commercial grade appliances, or in both, satisfy your needs and at the same time keep the kitchen quieter, cooler and safer by choosing from a growing number of specially engineered, adapted or commercial-type appliances for the home.

These "restaurant quality" appliances evolved from commercial equipment that's been redesigned and refined for residential use, in many cases by manufacturers of a commercial equipment line. As such, these refined restaurant-style units often include the best of both worlds—the versatility, speed and control of commercial appliances and the safety features required of residential equipment.

Adapted, styled, and/or redesigned commercial cooking appliances should satisfy the working needs of most serious cooks. And adapted or redesigned commercial appliances offer some necessary safety features that true commercial units don't, especially when it comes to ranges.

To begin with, residentially adapted cooking products are better insulated than their commercial cousins. This means that less heat escapes into living areas; the oven recovers an exact temperature faster after it's been opened; and the outside surfaces of the stove remain cooler to the touch, posing less of a hazard to the cook and others who might come in contact with surfaces.

Ranges adapted for residential use feature childproof safety knobs that must be pushed in and then turned so the burners cannot be lit accidentally, a feature not offered on ranges manufactured for the commercial market and one most important in homes with small children. Many commercially styled residential units feature electric or electronic ignition devices. Unlike the constantly burning pilots on commercial units, these save gas and thus money.

On the subject of kitchen design, it's important to realize that the larger burners on the commercially styled ranges generally mean the unit is deeper than the standard residential range, measuring about 31 or 32 inches. Since standard kitchen countertops are 24 to 25 inches deep, either the range will extend beyond the base cabinet fronts or custom countertops must be constructed. If you opt to purchase one of the smaller-scale, commercial-style ranges you'll lose the benefit of the extra space between burners.

Ranges styled along commercial lines offer larger burners than residential units. And there are more of them—typically six, or perhaps four burners and a grill/griddle. Whatever the burner configuration, the amount of heat generated, the British thermal units, or Btus, per hour on an adapted range is generally double, or in some cases triple, that of a regular residential unit, giving off anywhere from about 6,000–15,000 Btus per hour, still considerably less than true commercial equipment. That means another important consideration may be the need to purchase, if you don't already own them, heavy-duty, commercial-grade cooking equipment specifically designed for use at those higher temperatures.

Commercially styled residential ranges frequently feature stainless-steel and/or baked-enamel surfaces and extra large ovens, some with adjustable shelves. Some offer a broiler option in the oven.

Newer options on the commercially styled cooking equipment scene include dual-fuel ranges with gas burners and a self-cleaning, convection-mode electric oven, all in the same unit as well as small two-burner cooktop units that can be used in conjunction with a traditional cooktop.

Refrigerator/freezer combinations are the new kid on the block when it comes to commercial-grade products that have been adapted for residential use. While most of the manufacturers who produce them have been around for decades, residentially adapted commercial refrigerators, refrigerator/freezers and specially designed wine coolers have generally only been readily available on the consumer level for the last two decades or so.

Refrigeration units adapted from commercial lines for use in the home offer heavy-duty compressors, door gaskets and hinges as well as accurate humidity and temperature controls that gourmet cooks use to keep high-quality ingredients at their peak longer. Residentially adapted refrigeration units are bolstered with added sound-deadening insulation.

In terms of kitchen design, perhaps the most important adaptation of commercial refrigerators for home use is their depth. Twenty-four inches has fast become the industry standard because it means that the refrigerator matches the depth of standard base cabinets. Whether a high-tech, stainless-steel unit or one fitted with decorative wood or laminate panels to match cabinetry, the refrigerator blends into the kitchen, allowing the cabinetry or other feature to become the focal point, an important feature for those considering the looks of the finished kitchen space.

The shallow depth has another practical application: It makes it easier to locate stored items because the entire depth of the shelf can be seen. Adjustable shelves, automatic defrosters and ice makers, self-closing pullout bins, stainless-steel interiors and glass doors are some of the available options on refrigeration units.

After all these cautions, it's not much consolation to the average buyer to learn that there are no hard and fast nationally accepted codes on the proper installation of adapted commercial kitchen appliances. If you do succumb to the lure, be sure to check with local building officials to see exactly what the codes in your area require before you order. For the best advice, consult with professionals—an architect or kitchen designer, your builder or remodeling contractor, and most important, your local building inspector.

Microwave Ovens

Microwave oven features, like those of other small electronic goods, change constantly. In recent years, the "must have" microwave (reportedly used in 95% of kitchen remodels in 1993, according to the earlier mentioned NKBA survey) has evolved into a sophisticated time-saver that offers features such as child lockout systems. These operate via a simple numerical sequence (for example, push nine four times) to disable the cooking power. Some models offer a display that indicates the lock is activated. Many microwaves now feature pre-programmed, one-touch keys for frequently prepared foods such as popcorn or frozen pizza. Others offer turntables that eliminate the need to stop and stir, short cycles for quick reheating, automatic defrosting and an add-a-minute setting. At the upper end of the price spectrum (starting at around $450) you'll find units that combine microwave and convection cooking capabilities. These can be used as a straight convection oven, a microwave or in a combination of both modes to crisp and brown food while using less energy and keeping the kitchen cooler.

Microwave oven sizes are generally classified as compact at 0.6 cubic feet and under 600 watts, mid- or family size from 0.8 cu ft to about 1.0 cu ft with 700–800 watts, and full or large size from 1.1 cu ft and more with wattage from 900 on up to 1,100. Be sure to select an oven that will perform the functions your family will use.

The wattage of a microwave determines the oven's power and, therefore, the cooking time. The exterior dimensions of the oven will affect where in your kitchen you can locate it. The interior dimensions affect what you can cook in it: a tray of lasagna, several ears of corn, etc. (It's a good idea to shop for a new microwave with your favorite lasagna pan or casserole dish measurements along with you.)

Prices vary from manufacture to manufacturer, but generally, the more wattage and the more features, the more you should be prepared to spend. Expect the average microwave oven to last about seven to ten years. After that time it becomes prohibitively costly to repair. And by then manufacturers will have come out with a whole new round of features and options.

Look for exterior styling that offers an integrated assembly, with fewer cracks or crevices to collect grease and dirt, and easy-to-read controls. Wood grain models have all but disappeared, and white on white, black on black or almond on almond dominate.

Where to locate the microwave? That decision is best based on who the primary users are and what they use the oven for. If the primary cook uses the microwave during meal preparation, then locate it within, or close to, the main work triangle. If the kids use it to make popcorn and snacks, the best location might be out of the main work area, perhaps in a snack center close to the refrigerator or pantry. No matter where you decide to place the microwave, plan at least 15 inches of counter space above, below or adjacent to it. Install the unit so the bottom of the oven is anywhere from 24 inches to 48 inches above the floor, according to the NKBA design guidelines. Again, the exact height should be determined by what's most comfortable for the primary user.

Laundry

Manufacturers report a trend toward moving laundry equipment up and out of the basement and into the living areas where most of the laundry is generated. This move saves steps and valuable time. If you, like many, opt for the kitchen as the new location for your laundry equipment, factors such as styling and a color that bends with your kitchen decor could be top priorities. Consider models that feature sound-deadening insulation, especially if the kitchen is an open plan. In smaller kitchens, where space is at a premium, take a look at the stackable pairs or one-piece combination units now offered. Most occupy only a little more than a two-foot square of floor space, with no sacrifice in capacity. On the downside, if you choose this type of unit, both appliances must be replaced when one gives out. Before ordering any appliance, and especially a stackable unit, measure doorways, corners and halls on the way to its permanent home to make sure the appliance will fit through.

Of Note: A new round of Department of Energy use standards aimed at laundry equipment will be released in 1998. It will mandate how much energy washers can use. Since most of the energy is used to heat the water, expect the next generation of laundry equipment to use less water than ever before.

In recent years there's been renewed interest in front-loading, or horizontal-axis, models. At this writing, all European manufacturers and at least one U.S. manufacturer (White Westinghouse, under several labels) offer front loaders. Horizontal-axis washers contain no agitator and provide the mechanical action necessary to clean clothes by tumbling them through the water. As a rule, this type of washer requires less detergent and bleach and uses less water, and therefore, less energy to heat the water. And, because it has no agitator, a horizontal-axis machine is gentler on clothing. Though the interior tub may appear smaller, a horizontal-axis unit may actually hold the same volume of clothing as a larger machine with an agitator. Horizontal-axis machines can be installed under the kitchen counter. Two caveats: Once you start a cycle in a horizontal-axis machine, you can't open it to drop in a forgotten item. And the horizontal-axis machines currently available require more stooping and bending to load and unload, though manufacturers are right now in the process of developing top-loading horizontal-axis units.

The size and makeup of your family affects the size of the loads washed, which has a bearing on what model best suits your needs. For efficient laundering action as well as fabric protection, the clothes must tumble freely, which means you should select laundry equipment according to the volume, not necessarily the weight, of the items you wash on a regular basis. A small family of two might put a large capacity model to good use if they wear and wash lots of jeans, sweats or heavy work overalls, or use king-sized bedding and extra large bath towels.

Before you make a final selection on laundry equipment, take into consideration how often you do laundry. Those who, by preference or habit, launder a load a day might not require as large a machine as those who limit laundry day to once a week. Make sure you match washer and dryer capacity. A large-load washer and a small-capacity dryer could create laundry headaches.

As with other major appliance purchases, the features on the laundry pair vary widely from a basic model to something one step up and finally the high-end model. Fabric softener and bleach dispensers, a self-cleaning lint filter, timer, heat sensors, delayed start, partial fills, hand-wash cycles, extra rinses, sound-deadening insulation, a stainless-steel tub or cabinet, electronic touch controls and front service panels are among the items that quickly add to the cost, but also to the convenience and sometimes to the performance of a unit. For example, the ability to preprogram your favorite cycle makes it easier for the kids to help with the laundry. Timers that count down the time left on a cycle allow you to get one more chore or errand done rather than stand around waiting for the washer or dryer cycle to finish.

Speaking of cycles, the more cycles a model offers, the higher the price tag. For example, a two-speed washer provides a delicate cycle that one-speed models don't offer. And a three-speed unit can create a hand-wash simulation, with a brief agitation, then a rest of a few seconds, then more agitation. Be sure to consider the types of clothing your family owns. With the proliferation of natural fibers in use today, a hand-wash cycle could prolong the life of your favorite pieces. And a permanent press cycle, which washes in warm water and then rinses in cold, cools fibers so they contract and thus wrinkle less.

Study the yellow energy-efficiency use labels (see Chapter 5, Environmental Concerns, page 45) on washers. (Dryers don't carry them.) They calculate the estimated cost or running individual models. Frequently, a higher initial "sticker price" is offset by the anticipated energy cost savings over the life span of a particular model. Washer prices start at about $250 for the most basic models and go on up to more than $2,000 for a deluxe European model, depending on the manufacturer and the features. Dryers begin at about $250 and range on up to more than $2,500. Plan to pay slightly more (about $50) for a gas dryer with the same features as an electric model because there are more components in a gas dryer. Again, plan to recoup that in energy cost savings over the lifetime of the dryer.

CHAPTER 10

Finishing Touches

*(How to Add Personality—Yours
. . . Not the Designer's)*

Some people thrive in a kitchen that's cluttered, they are happiest and most productive when surrounded by items they cherish or objects that inspire them. Others can't function if there's so much as a teaspoon out of place. Some folks evidence a fondness for any shade of blue, while others consider only yellow. And then there are those who insist on pristine white everywhere. Many feel most at home surrounded with colorful, splashy prints or bold geometrics. Others opt for dainty florals and neat checks and plaids. Some prefer rich contrast, while others are most comfortable in a softly blended monochromatic room.

If you've never thought much about your own particular kitchen decorating likes and dislikes, the planning phase of a remodel is a good time to begin. When you take the time to sort out and apply your decorating preferences, you're bound to create a room that's comfortable and feels like home. You are investing a great deal of thought and time, not to mention money, into your project. The end result might as well fit you like a custom-made suit.

In the Beginning

Think of the architecture as the basis, or bones, of your space. Just as your skeleton provides the framework for your face and body type, size and shape, the architecture provides the framework for the eventual look of your kitchen. The collective impact of the shape of the room, the size and placement of windows and doors, along with the presence (or absence) of items such as layered or carved moldings, skylights, exposed beams, a fireplace, chair rail or window seat provide the foundation for your decorating scheme. If your space doesn't contain anything that could be construed as an architectural detail, now is the time to consider adding some as space and budget allow. Architectural details set the general decorating tone of a space; i.e., soaring ceilings and skylights suggest one finished look; multipaned windows, a brick or natural stone fireplace and exposed beams, another.

The style of the cabinetry you select will take you a long way toward defining the look of your kitchen. Glossy red or textured gray laminate cabinets will always suggest a sleek, contemporary space. Wood, on the other hand, can project an image of rich tradition (cherry) or relaxed ease (pine or oak), or light and bright contemporary (birch or ash), depending on the door style you select and the wood you choose.

Many people claim they have no real decorating preferences. "Anything is bound to be better than what we have" and "Just as long as it's not dark, I'll be happy" are familiar refrains. Yet a careful study of your growing clipping collection should indicate the cabinetry look and material that most often caught your eye and offer another clue to solving the how-to-decorate mystery.

A glance back at your lifestyle questionnaire (in the first chapter) can also help further define your interior decorating style, even if you never thought you had one. Keep your top remodeling or building priority in mind when choosing finishing materials, and a decorating direction begins to emerge almost effortlessly. For example, if part of your motivation for designing a new kitchen is to create an easy-to-maintain space, you might decide to eliminate harder-to-maintain colors, such as white, in favor of a soft pastel gray or a textured pastel laminate, neither of which shows every fingerprint. If your aim is to create a warm and homey family gathering space, then traditional materials such as wood, ceramic tile or natural stone ought to be included.

Once you've noted the basic architecture of the space and the style you prefer in cabinets, the remainder of the interior design of the space depends on the finishing materials you select and the details you add.

Create the Look You Want

While there is no one right way or single set of components that make up each style, there are some guidelines to follow:

The key to creating a traditional kitchen is to choose formal, elegant components. Cabinetry with a white or light finish on a tight-grained wood with a raised panel door is a good choice. Or pick a neat, tight-grained dark wood cabinet, such as cherry, and accent with brass or pewter hardware. Add a few well-placed cabinets with mullioned glass doors that will allow you to display collectibles or heirlooms. Choose uniform-width, slim planks for the floor. Avoid floors with strong grains— the style is too rugged for this formal look. Finish off with decorative crown moldings.

Clean lines are the hallmark of the contemporary look. That doesn't mean you must stick to hard edges. Soften the edges of a contemporary room with curved doors on cabinetry and countertops. Choose wood cabinets with plain, sleek, full-overlay doors finished with a wash that lets the grain of the wood show. Or go with dark and dramatic laminate colors or a red-toned cherry door that's trimmed in ebony. Select minimalist hardware. Choose a bright floor that's part of the fun of the design, or minimize the importance of the floor by going with a neutral color.

American country is a simple, warm, straightforward look that calls for flat-panel style cabinet doors in white-painted wood or a light to medium natural finish. Or look for cabinets in "distressed" or aged woods. Here's where wide random plank floors work best. Or opt for a painted, checkerboard or stenciled floor. For hardware, choose white porcelain, pewter, or simple wood knobs that match the cabinets.

Choose a Color Scheme

Selecting a color you can live with for years to come can seem like one of the most confounding parts of decorating your new kitchen. If you find it a daunting task, you're not alone. Begin narrowing your choices by studying the contents of your clothes closet. That's right—your clothes closet. Because the colors you wear well and often are most likely the colors that look best on you. Therefore they, and their close relatives, will look great around you too.

Should your favorite color happen to be a bright and forceful shade of teal, sunshine yellow, or fuchsia, plan to use it in accent touches scattered throughout the space in small doses, such as in the ceramic tile backsplash. Or in soft goods, such as window treatments, seat cushions and other items that can be replaced at a later date if you tire of them or your tastes change. Or plunge in and paint, not paper, the walls with a shade of your absolute favorite. If you tire of it, or decide it really is too strong, repainting is always an option.

Follow the tried-and-true decorating hint and use a color scheme inspired by a favorite fabric, wall covering or painting. That's easier than ever now that computer matching has entered into color selections. You won't need to rely on your untrained eye to make a color selection if you find a local paint store that offers (usually free) computer color matching services. Take in swatches, with bits of the color you want to match that total at least the size of a quarter, and the computer will read the color and create a formula for the paint.

Or choose a color that complements the ceramic tile or laminate countertops you've chosen, or one that brightens a naturally dark space or visually expands a small one.

Of Note: Scientists have known for years that certain colors trigger a specific emotional response in people. Each color has a personality that combines with your own to evoke a certain feeling or mood. In the course of his work over the years, Kenneth Charbonneau, director of color marketing at Benjamin Moore & Co., observes that:

White is crisp, clean, classical, timeless and pure. White lies are benign. There is no such thing as just plain white. All whites contain a hint of color whether it's soft, rosy pink or cool gray; it's there if you look.

Red is the first color perceived by babies. Red quickens the heartbeat, prompts the release of adrenaline into the bloodstream and provides a sense of warmth. Red overrules all surrounding colors and stands out in a crowd. Red is associated with passion, anger and rage.

Yellow is the color of the sun, which gives life, and of gold, the measure of earthly riches. It is cheerful, but not flattering to most complexions or eyes. It's the predominant color of spring flowers (think daffodils, crocus, forsythia) and it's used as a warning color for heavy machinery, and on school buses. Yellow is also associated with jaundice and cowardice.

Green, the color of foliage and the new life of spring, is also associated with mold and decay. Green is the most restful color to the eye. It's also the color of camouflage and of money.

Blue is the color of the sky and the ocean. It's the historical symbol of royalty and authority. Police most often wear blue uniforms. Blue chip means the highest quality, blue blood the high born, and blue ribbon is the winner. But feeling blue is no fun. It looks as though blue denim will never go out of style.

Tricks for Adding Personality

• Apply a faux paint technique to create texture or visual interest. Some techniques, such as sponging, ragging and color washing, are definitely easy enough to execute yourself. Or commission an artist to create a trompe l'oeil masterpiece. Possibilities include creating a view where none exists via a faux window; a peek through an archway into a country garden or down a narrow, winding, cobble-lined city street lined with quaint shops.

• Stencil a border on walls or floors. Cut your own, buy a ready-made precut template, or hire an artist to design and/or implement a pattern you can collaborate on designing. Stencil designs can suit traditional, country or even contemporary spaces. Be sure to allow sufficient drying time between coats of paint. And plan to protect your freshly painted floor with two or even three coats of polyurethane.

• Add an herb patch. Gardeners might consider adding a greenhouse window large enough to sustain a few pots of favorite herbs in a year-round indoor garden or to provide a home for an ever-changing display of bulbs and seasonal flowers. A ceramic tile or solid-surfacing windowsill handles the inevitable drips from watering. In areas with long, dark winters, plan sufficient recessed lighting in the window well to accommodate plant lights.

• Personalize the backsplash. Often forgotten, it's an area you'll view from every angle of the room. Create a tile mural. Select from one of the many hand-painted ceramic tile murals available on a stock basis from a local tile showroom, or order a custom-designed mural from one of the companies who specialize in creating one-of-a-kind, hand-painted, made-to-order tiles. Depending on the size of your new kitchen, you might need only splurge on a dozen or so decorative tiles to scatter in a field of plain tiles set in the backsplash or countertop. Choose from both realistic or fanciful designs that include colorful fruits, flowers and ferns, vegetables, land and sea animals and other naturally inspired motifs. Or brighten things up with the strong contrast of a few primary or other brightly colored tiles set in a white or neutral field. Experiment with sizes and shapes to create geometric borders and patterns.

• Use the floor as part of the decor. Personalize wood floors by installing them on the diagonal or by adding a contrasting border or corner medallions. Some of the newer sheet vinyl flooring products can combine in interesting ways to define different areas and to create visual interest. Consider installing large 1-foot-square ceramic tiles of a single color on the diagonal. Or alternate diagonally laid white or light tiles with a contrasting dark for a timeless look that suits both traditional and contemporary spaces.

Combine ceramic tile with wood on floors for a personal touch. Adapt a favorite motif to create a tile "carpet" in the center of the space, in front of the fireplace or under the breakfast table. A durable tile "runner" installed in front of the cabinets in the main work area works well with hardwood floors in the remainder of the space. And the tile stands up to the wear and tear of constant traffic and never needs refinishing.

• Countertop materials and colors as well as inlays and one-of-a kind decorative edge treatments can add personality to your space. Since it's a small area, it's a great place to play with color and not overwhelm the space.

- Even the smallest items add interest. Case in point: cabinetry hardware. Available in a variety of styles ranging from discreet china knobs to bold brass, chunky solid-surfacing pulls and exquisite handmade pulls, the tiny details of hardware can make an enormous contribution to the overall look of your kitchen. You'll find styles that range from high-tech to antique in finishes that include metal, wood, porcelain, plastic and faux stone solid-surfacing materials. Function counts too, so test the hardware you are considering for comfort and ease of operation before you buy.

- If you own three or more of anything, you've got a collection. And there's nothing like an artfully displayed grouping of your favorite objects to instantly imbue a room with your personality. Why not display the collection in the kitchen, the room where you likely spend most of your time?

Collections needn't be rare, useless, expensive or antique. If you don't happen to collect antique cooking implements, interesting teapots, fine hand-painted china cups and saucers, mustache cups, or porridge dishes, then plan a prominent space to display your cookbooks or Grandma's charming hand-me-down china. Framed artwork—everything from your own collages or photographs to the children's or grandchildren's finger-paintings, to pieces you purchase especially for the room from a local gallery or poster shop—is a possibility.

Don't have a collection? Think about starting one. If that seems too frivolous, collect items that you can make use of in or about the kitchen, such as pottery coffee mugs in a favorite color or motif, in different sizes and shapes. They'll not only come in handy on an everyday basis but could be used when entertaining large groups. So could serving dishes or platters in a particular pattern or with a common motif, or a variety of shapes and sizes of yellow vases, or grape-patterned pitchers or hand-woven baskets with handles.

If your collection won't be used on a regular basis, plan to store it inside cabinets behind clear glass doors. A note of caution: If you opt for a cabinet door style with mullions (bars that cross the face of the glass in a decorative pattern), you'll need to be sure the shelves, as arranged, line up with those decorative bars to avoid visual clutter. Measure the various items you plan to display to be sure they will fit on the shelves before ordering the cabinetry.

No matter what your collection is or how you decide to display it, think about adding extra lighting, such as spots, to focus more attention there.

• Fabric provides the perfect opportunity to bring your personality to a kitchen space. Add touches of your favorites on banquettes or chair cushions, or in window treatments. Vintage table linens and dish towels convert to interesting, personalized window treatments. A collection of old buttons could be used as tabs on new window treatments.

• Still don't have a decorative starting point? Need inspiration? Pay a visit to your local wall covering retailer. You won't have trouble finding a style or colorway that suits you. On the contrary, the most difficult part of your selection will probably be homing in on the one pattern you like best.

One fabulous wall covering is a great starting point to create a look, no matter what the style of your kitchen. Choose from the wide array of pre-coordinated collections. And study the wall covering sample books for ideas. Don't limit yourself to a single pattern applied only to the walls. Border windows or accent a soffit. Create architectural interest where none exists by using a border to separate two different but coordinated patterns, one above, one below, for a chair-rail effect. Use a wall covering border to edge open shelves. Apply borders down both walls at the corners of the room. Consider covering the ceiling for a jewel-box effect. One hint: If you are using a border to frame a window, choose a nondirectional pattern. Select a line that includes coordinated fabrics for window treatments, seat covers, place mats and table linens. Limit your choices to washable vinyls from the precoordinated collections that include companion papers, fabrics and borders, and you'll be taking advantage of the manufacturer's free interior design assistance.

If you take the time necessary to identify and clarify your decorating preferences now, you're bound to create a kitchen that suits you perfectly and is as personalized as your face and fingerprints.

CHAPTER 11

Working With the Pros

*(The Whys and Hows of Working
With Design Professionals)*

If all that you know about cars could fit neatly on the head of a pin, when yours breaks down, you probably call on a competent mechanic. And when your bad back or your allergies flare up, it's likely you see the best doctor you can find. It stands to reason then that if your kitchen is poorly laid out, or hopelessly outdated, when it comes time to remodel, you'll hire a design professional to walk you through the process of designing your new space. Or will you?

For a variety of reasons, many homeowners are unwilling to call on an architect, interior designer, space planner or kitchen designer for assistance with a building or remodeling project. Some defend their reluctance because they believe hiring a design professional will add to the cost of the project. Or they believe that professionals will only work on high-end projects. "I'm on a budget and can't afford a designer." Or, "We don't want anything complicated, so we don't need a designer." But a competent and thorough design professional who prevents just one potentially costly error or who knows where you can purchase the range, ventilation and lighting you've seen in magazines and have your heart set on, or who solves the puzzle for the best location for the microwave, range or sink to maximize your available space and improves the function of the plan, earns his/her fee by saving you not only time and money but also stress, frustration and aggravation.

Other homeowners protest that they prefer to undertake the design themselves. "This is my kitchen, and I don't want any designer telling me what to do." Or, "I'm perfectly capable of designing my own kitchen." These are the same people who fear they'll lose control of the look, not to mention the budget, for their new kitchen. But no professional designer worth the price of the paper his/her portfolio is printed on will insist that you use chartreuse if you hate chartreuse, or wood if you want laminate, or an electric range if you want gas. Professional designers do rely on their experience with a wide variety of products to make recommendations and provide information about which items they believe will function optimally, or perhaps not at all, in your space and suit your lifestyle.

There are homeowners who argue that "no one could possibly know my kitchen like I do." That's precisely why a thorough professional designer will visit your present kitchen and ask what seems like hundreds of questions (similar to those found in Chapter 1, What's a Lifestyle Anyway?, page 1) and even note your height and the length of your reach, all in order to glean all the information he/she needs to help you decide what to include where in a new kitchen. It will be your answers to questions about your needs, budget, lifestyle and preferences, when combined with the design professional's knowledge of products, construction, safety and codes plus his/her training and creativity, that forms the basis of your new kitchen design.

Still other homeowners are under the impression that they can rely on their remodeling contractor or builder to design a *maximally functional* kitchen. In most cases, this is simply not true. Yes, most builders and remodeling contractors have vast experience measuring and installing the various components of a kitchen. Yes, they can provide an idea of the cost and durability of products and of the whereabouts and reliability of local suppliers. Yes, they may even provide a working kitchen plan with functional materials and layout. But few remodeling contractors and new home builders or, for that matter, interior designers and architects, are *specifically trained* to consider the finer points of kitchen design, or have the product knowledge necessary to create a maximally functional and truly personalized kitchen design. If you decide to depend on any design professional for kitchen design solutions, ask if he or she has any *kitchen design* training. Is he or she aware of the latest ergonomic research and NKBA guidelines for kitchen design? Of work centers and how they function? How many kitchens has he/she designed?

Of Note: Effective kitchen design is an enormously detailed undertaking, which means that the path to the perfect kitchen layout is fraught with many potential pitfalls. For example, if you undertake the project yourself and measure incorrectly and then order products based on those measurements, you face the prospect of returning the products, delaying the project while you wait for replacements, and possibly paying hefty restocking fees. And that's the best-case scenario. Some special order products may not be returnable. It's doubtful that a design or building professional would make this type of error. And if they did, they would be responsible for rectifying the situation.

How to Find a Designer

The easiest and surest way to find a design professional is, of course, through a personal referral. Ask everyone you know if they have worked with a kitchen designer, architect, or other design professional they would recommend. Peruse both national, and especially regional, magazines for the work of local designers. Check the credits at the back of the magazine to see if any of the designers featured are in your area. Put in a call to the design trade associations and ask for referrals in your area. (See Resources, page 144, for telephone numbers.) Attend local builders' open houses and ask for the name of the kitchen designer they worked with. Often the kitchens of decorator showhouses feature the work of talented, top-notch local designers. Pay a visit to the home show in your area and seek out the dealers who are showcasing products there. Look for courses on interior design or kitchen planning at community adult education centers. Such courses are often taught by designers who are eager to connect with new clients. Finally, take a look in the local newspaper and the Yellow Pages under "Kitchen Cabinets" and "Kitchen Remodeling." You'll find prospects galore to consider.

When you've honed in on the type of professional you would like to work with, set up an interview. Ask about training and experience. How long has he/she been in business? How long does he/she anticipate that the job will take? When can he/she start? Ask for references on projects that are similar in size and scope to yours. And don't just file the references. Check them out. If possible, take the time to go to see a project or two personally. Ask specific questions. Was the work started on time? Did the project stay on schedule? Within budget? What ideas and solutions came from the designer? Did the clients have any particular problems? Would they work with this design professional again?

No matter which type of professional you decide to work with, don't consider hiring anyone you don't have a rapport with. You'll be spending a great deal of time with this person over the course of your project, particularly in the case of new construction or a major remodel. You need to feel free to express your opinion, ask questions and perhaps even voice complaints. If you can't communicate openly and comfortably with each other, you probably have the wrong designer. Keep looking.

Be honest and open about your budget. There's no point in wasting your time or the designer's sending him/her off to sketch out a kitchen plan executed with $50,000 worth of custom-made cabinetry and high-end appliances if your true top line is $20,000. Good design is good design. And one of the biggest advantages for working with a design professional is that their knowledge of alternatives can help you to stay within your budget. A well-thought out floor plan can be executed with low, medium or high-end products. (See Chapter 3, Holding the Budget Line, page 25.) Be aware that many kitchen and bath showrooms and/or cabinetmakers offer a product line that addresses just one market niche. Others carry several product lines meant to satisfy needs across the board. So don't get your heart set on using the high-end firm in town if the products they carry to execute their designs don't fit into your budget plans.

You'll need to provide the design professional you choose to work with an idea of what you like, even if you're not sure exactly what that is or what you want. A good place to start: Share your clipping file. And ask to see their portfolio of before-and-after shots of projects.

How they make their money varies, depending on the firm or the type of designer you decide to work with. Professional designers are paid for their time in a variety of ways: Many architects work on a percentage of the construction cost for the project, an hourly rate, or a lump sum payment. Often interior designers or kitchen designers are paid a commission on the component parts or a flat, fixed fee that's set in advance. Some kitchen designers work independently and will supply just the design, or supply the design and supervise the construction. Design building firms handle it all and incorporate their design fee into the total cost of the project. Don't ignore this all-important issue. Ask about payment practices at the time of your initial meeting.

The Various Pros and What They Know

If you do decide to enlist the aid of a design professional, there are several options open to you. Remember: There are designers and then there are designers. No matter what category of professional you may call in, ask specifically about his/her training and/or experience in kitchen design.

Many kitchen and bath showrooms, cabinet shops and some home centers are staffed by kitchen and bath and/or interior designers. Again, don't take it for granted that the person selling cabinetry or appliances has received special kitchen planning training. Ask.

There are some 1,500 designers who have earned certification in their field. These Certified Kitchen Designers (CKDs) are scattered throughout the U.S. and Canada. Most work for, or are the owners of, cabinetry showrooms or kitchen dealerships, but some work independently. Their certification process includes courses and/or seminars in not only design and the fundamentals of what goes into a kitchen but in measuring, drawing, ergonomics, etc. Before one can sit for the seven-hour-long CKD qualifying exam, he/she must have seven years (or the equivalent) of full-time kitchen design experience and/or education and must demonstrate ability by presenting two samples of work and two client references. CKDs must report ongoing professional development that includes seminars, attendance at trade shows and the like in order to retain certification once it's earned. To locate a Certified Kitchen Designer near you, call NKBA or check the local Yellow Pages.

As of 1998, CKDs will also be required to pass the National Council of Interior Design Qualifications, which in turn requires a minimum of a two-year design degree. The American Society of Interior Designers (ASID), International Society of Interior Designers (ISID) and the Interior Designers of Canada (IDC) all require professional members to meet rigorous standards, including full-time work experience or accredited education in addition to passing the two-day National Council for Interior Design Qualifications (NCIDQ). The impartial, third-party administered examination tests an individual's minimum competency in interior design. Interior designers' qualifications vary. A growing number of states and all Canadian provinces require interior designers to be licensed. Again, a license does not specifically equate to kitchen design experience. Ask.

The recently established Residential Space Planners International's members must undergo an oral portfolio presentation to earn professional status in this international performance-based organization. Space planners are problem-solvers and organizers who aim to create functional, intelligently designed and aesthetic environments, including kitchens, through the use of problem-solving methods and design criteria. Their work is reviewed by a five-member board for adherence to accepted space planning and design principles, codes and clearances as well as aesthetics. And they must submit client and trade affiliate letters of recommendation. Call RSPI (see Resources, page 144) national headquarters for the space planner nearest you.

Architects are licensed by the state where they practice after earning a degree, participating in a formal internship, and passing a four-day test, the Architectural Registration Exam. Architecture programs follow an established curriculum supervised by the accrediting body and include a minimum of 50 hours of design courses (not necessarily involving the kitchen) as well as structural and mechanical engineering, environmental science, contracts and psychology.

An architect can design your project and supervise everything from start to finish or just supply you with a design. But since, in many states, they are professionally responsible for the construction work, don't expect an architect to affix a professional license seal unless they will be supervising the construction. If not, what you'll end up with instead is a preliminary or a schematic. This type of a builder plan is a recommendation, not a design the architect will necessarily be responsible for. The laws governing responsibility for the construction vary from region to region.

With about 100,000 architects in the U.S., a personal reference is the best way to find one. State registration boards will give you a list of all architects in the state, or check the Yellow Pages. The American Institute of Architects (AIA) is a professional society (see Resources, page 144); as such, membership is voluntary, there is no qualifying examination or certification, and not all architects belong. Each state chapter of AIA does maintain a listing of member firms. Call for a referral in your area. Many architects, however, do not focus on the details of kitchen design. Some work with Certified Kitchen Designers or can recommend one. First question when you call an architectural firm: Do they handle residential projects?

Membership in The National Association of Home Builders (NAHB) National Remodelers™ Council, a trade association (see Resources, page 144), provides a badge of credibility and is a good indicator that this remodeling professional takes business seriously. The group began a Certified Graduate Remodeler program in 1991, and by 1996 it's anticipated there will be 100 CGRs throughout the country. Qualifications are strict and involve a lengthy process during which insurance is verified and the remodeler is required to take as many as nine business courses covering estimating, sales and marketing, along with some design. But none focus on kitchen design specifically. CGRs must update their certification every three years with new courses.

The National Association of the Remodeling Industry (NARI) is a 50-year-old trade association (see Resources, page 144) made up of more than 6,000 member companies who are serious enough about their businesses to pay the association dues and who agree to conduct their businesses according to NARI's recommended practices. Some NARI members go on to earn the group's Certified Remodeler (CR) designation for general construction work or Certified Remodeler Specialist (CRS) designation for specialized contractors such as ceramic tile and marble installers, electricians, masons, etc. In order to earn either certification, members must have at least five years of experience in the remodeling business, detail their background and experience in writing, adhere to the group's standards of practice and code of ethics, and pass a comprehensive written examination based on knowledge of construction and business practices and that includes current kitchen design standards. While they are serious businessmen, NARI members are not required to take courses in kitchen design. Again, ask.

Contact any one of these trade associations or professional groups, and you'll be well on your way to finding a building professional who can help to turn your dream kitchen plans into reality.

Of Note: You may have noticed a proliferation of kitchen floor plan software on the shelves during your last trip to the computer or office supply store. These programs, priced from about $10 to $75, are one convenient way to test out a variety of layouts and to develop a preliminary plan. But, like a word processing program you could use to write a best-selling novel only if you possess the skill, talent and imagination to do so, a space planning software program won't help you design a great kitchen if you don't have a thorough knowledge of the design principles involved. Such software programs are only as good as the designer manipulating them. They do not alert you to safety rules or to building code requirements, nor are they based on the NKBA guidelines for functional kitchen design. They do not take the place of a thorough and knowledgeable design professional to develop or to review your plan.

The "Can-I-Go-It-Alone?" Quiz

Still not convinced to hire a design pro, or at the very least to hire a professional to critique your plan? Here's a simple test of the depth of your knowledge about kitchen design details. If you can answer all five questions, you probably possess enough basic knowledge to plan your new kitchen without the aid of a design professional. However, if you are unable to answer even one of the questions, you could end up facing schedule-snafuing, not to mention expensive, design glitches in your new kitchen plan that will require last-minute installation changes and/or reduce the function and efficiency over the lifetime of the room.

1. A 30-inch-wide sink requires a sink base cabinet that is

    A. the same size.
    B. 3 inches wider than the sink.
    C. 6 inches wider than the sink.

2. The joists under your kitchen run parallel with:

    A. the length of the room.
    B. the width of the room.

3. The vent stack for the kitchen plumbing is located _____.

4. In order to operate most effectively, the ventilation unit above the range should be:

    A. wider than the range by 3 inches.
    B. wider than the range by 6 inches.
    C. the same width as the range.

5. A standard refrigerator requires no less than $\frac{1}{2}$ inch, 1 inch, or 2 inches of clearance on each side?

Answers:

1. **B.** Why is this important? Choose too small a base, and the sink may not fit into it. Go back to start while you wait for the reordered sink. Or the plumber may need twice as much time to install the sink, both of which could cost you extra money.

2. The answer could be either A or B. If you mess up on this one, you may not be able to install the downdrafted cooktop you dreamed about and paid for. The direction the joists run in affects where you can locate the venting system for downdrafted cooking equipment.

3. If you make a mistake and plan your recessed pantry so that it interferes with pipes in the wall, you and the building inspector could become best buddies. And the plumber will be forever grateful for his two-week vacation in Tahiti.

4. **B.** A total of 6 inches wider than the range in order to capture as much steam, heat and odor as possible.

5. 1 inch of clearance on each side of the refrigerator will allow sufficient space to pull the refrigerator out of its niche to clean under and behind, the most crucial factor in refrigerator maintenance.

CHAPTER 12

Finale

(The Importance of the Kitchen in Your Home)

The kitchen is . . . the place where the family gathers to do just about everything.
Liesl B., Ocean Grove, NJ

The kitchen is . . . where I store my food and use the microwave, that is, when it's not functioning as my office.
Mary W., New York, NY

The kitchen is . . . my absolute favorite room because I love to cook.
Denise K., Chicago, IL

The kitchen is . . . an art gallery (for an eclectic collection of stuffed fish, framed photos and found objects) where I love to whip up weekend feasts for friends and family.
Russell S., Jersey City, NJ

The kitchen is . . . the easiest-to-clean room in my house and the place I can't wait to get out of so I can get into my garden, or the office, or my car, or anywhere else.
Claire W., Houston, TX

Ask any number of people to define what "kitchen" means to them and you're bound to hear any number of different answers. Because, in addition to its universal purpose as the food storage and preparation center of today's home, the modern kitchen nearly always fulfills many other functions.

No matter what your decorative style, or the size or location of your home, or the configuration of your family, it's likely that your kitchen probably plays a central role in daily life. "Not me," you might say. "I'm not a cook, so I get in and out of the kitchen as fast as I can." Consider this: Where does your family congregate to light the candles on the birthday cake, whether it's home-baked or store-bought? Where do you carve the Halloween pumpkin and prepare the Thanksgiving turkey and bake holiday treats? Be honest—where do your kids prefer to do their homework? Showcase their artwork? And where is it that you invariably handle all those necessary phone calls, juggle scheduling, and perhaps do the laundry, all while planning and/or preparing dinner? Where *do* all the best parties at your house end up?

If your family is anything like millions of others all over the world, your answer is probably "in the kitchen." For, from the moment man first brought fire indoors, the kitchen has functioned as the heart of the home. And now, despite the disappearance of the fire and the hearth from the majority of modern kitchens, it's still the room that remains the central core of most homes. Even with the existence of numerous alternatives, such as the living, family or great room, the den and/or the media center, it's most often the kitchen where families, in all their various modern configurations, gather together for at least part of each day. And not just to plan, to prepare and to eat meals. The kitchen is the favored location for sharing time, and perhaps a cup of tea or coffee with a friend. It's the room where family members are most likely to gather to exchange information and ideas, make plans, work out problems, arrange social events, do homework, or perhaps catch up on a hobby, a home-based business or volunteer work.

With that in mind, it's easy to see why the best time for you (and your family) to decide exactly how you want to define "kitchen" is during the planning phase of the design project. Take the time now to plan a kitchen that not only accommodates but actually encourages a number of the varied activities *your* family participates in. Now is the time to decide if your kitchen will function as the prime family gathering spot, as an easy-to-care-for snack center or an architectural showplace, a family mission-control center, a site for informal cooking parties with friends, as your own private gourmet cooking laboratory or as a yet unnamed and unclassified permutation of all, or any, of the above. For, with careful planning, it *is* possible to turn your kitchen into exactly the kind of space *your* family requires.

Take your time. Explore the many possibilities. Doodle your ideas on paper. Relax. Have fun and enjoy the process. Armed with the knowledge you've gained in these pages, feel confident that you're on your way to creating the kitchen of your dreams.

Resources

APPLIANCES

To obtain service information, repair manuals, parts orders, dealer referrals, warranty information or literature. Most numbers are answered 24 hours a day, every day of the week.

Amana 800-843-0304
Caloric 800-843-0304
Frigidaire 800-451-7007
General Electric 800-626-2000
Gibson 800-458-1445
Hotpoint 800-626-2000
Jenn-Air 800-668-1100
Kelvinator 800-323-7773
KitchenAid 800-422-1230
Maytag 800-688-9900
Modern Maid 800-843-0304
O'Keefe & Merritt 800-537-5530
RCA 800-626-2000
Roper 800-447-6737
Speed Queen 800-843-0304
Sub-Zero 800-444-7820
Tappan 800-537-5530

Whirlpool 800-253-1301
White Westinghouse 800-245-0600

CABINETS

Kitchen Cabinet Manufacturers Association
1899 Preston White Drive
Reston VA 22091
703-264-1690
directory of member manufacturers

CONSTRUCTION AND DESIGN EXPERTISE

American Institute of Architects (AIA)
1735 New York Ave N.W.
Washington DC 20006
202-626-7300
brochures, video on how to work with an architect on a remodeling project

American Lighting Association
World Trade Center
2050 Stemmons Freeway
P.O. Box 530168
Dallas TX 75258
800-274-4484

American Society of Interior
Designers (ASID)
608 Massachusetts Ave. N.E.
Washington DC 20002
800-775-ASID (2743)
Client/Designer Selection Service re-
quests are handled through national
office and forwarded on to the local
chapter nearest you.

Hardwood Manufacturers
Association
Department NEC
400 Penn Center Blvd.
Suite 530
Pittsburgh PA 15235
800-373-WOOD

International Association of
Lighting Designers
18 E. 16 Street
New York NY 10013
212-206-1281
referrals, brochure

Interior Designers of Canada
260 King Street E.
Suite 414
Toronto, Ontario M5A1K3
416-594-9310 for the provincial
office nearest you

NAHB Remodelers Council
1201 15th St. N.W.
Washington DC 20005
202-822-0451 send SASE for a 12-
page brochure, "How to Choose a
Remodeler Who's on the Level"

National Association of Plumbing,
Heating, Cooling Contractors
Education Foundation
P.O. Box 6808
Falls Church VA 22040-1148
800-533-7694

National Association of the
Remodeling Industry (NARI)
4301 North Fairfax Dr.
Suite 310
Arlington VA 22203-1627
for a free copy of a brochure enti-
tled "Select a Professional Remodeling Contractor" and a list of
NARI members in your area
800-440-NARI

National Kitchen & Bath
Association (NKBA)
687 Willowgrove St.
Hackettstown NJ 07840
For a copy of Universal Design
Guidelines:
800-FOR-NKBA (367-6522);
for NKBA member referral (not
necessarily a CKD); kitchen planning kit, $3:
800-401-NKBA (401-6522)

Residential Space Planners
International (RSPI)
P.O. Box 80243
San Marino CA 91108
818-284-2949

RECYCLING
Send for a free brochure about solid
waste recycling:
Recycling, Waste Management Inc.,
P.O. Box 11205, Dept. SS
Chicago IL 60611

Write to the National Recycling
Coalition, for general information
on starting a recycling program in
your area:
1101 30th St. N.W.
Suite 305
Washington DC 20007
202-625-6406

Request mail-order catalogues of
"green products" from:
The Energy Store
800-288-1938;
Energy Federation,
800-876-0660;
EcoSource,
800-274-7040;
Seventh Generation,
800-441-2538

UNIVERSAL DESIGN
Write for an Easy Access checklist
SASE to
Easy Access Housing
The National Easter Seal Society
70 East Lake St.
Chicago IL 60601
312-726-6200 ext. 5303

National Association of Home
Builders (NAHB)
National Research Center
400 Prince Georges Blvd.
Upper Marlboro MD 20772
301-249-4000
For information on designing bar-
rier-free, accessible homes, send $10
plus $3 to cover postage and han-
dling. Ask for the "Comprehensive
Approach to Retrofitting Homes for
a Lifetime" and a free publication
list that will provide other sources.

Index

accessibility, in kitchen design, 37–44
  adaptations for, 43
  information resources, 147
  lighting and, 43
  professional designers and, 38
  traffic flow and, 38
allergies, 89
American Institute of Architects (AIA), 137, 145
American Society of Interior Design (ASID), 136, 146
appliances, major. *See also types of appliances*
  accessible design of, 39–41
  commercial-type adaptations, 111–114
  cost of operating, 95
  costs of, 35
  energy use, 45, 47–48, 95–96, 98, 117, 118–119
  information resources, 145
  not skimping on costs of, 32–33, 96
  reasons for replacing, 95–96
  rules of thumb for choosing, 96–97
  warranties, 97
architects, licensed, 136–137
architecture, and decorating scheme, 122
Association of Home Appliance Manufacturers (AHAM), 95, 98

backsplashes
  ceramic tile, 59, 126–127
  defined, 58
  full-height, 65
  personalizing with ceramic tiles, 126
  solid-surfacing materials for, 59, 61
  surface materials, 42
bake centers, 21
budget. *See also* costs
  design professionals and, 131–132
  hypothetical examples, 35
  informing design professional about, 134–135
  realistic, setting and holding to, 25–35
butcher-block, for countertops, 62–63

cabinetry, 81–94
  accessible design, 41–42
  considerations in selecting, 94
  costs of, 81
  custom-made, 82–83
  cutting costs on, 33
  decorating preferences in, 122, 123–124
  for display of collections, 129
  frame versus frameless (Eurostyle), 83, 85
  in galley kitchens, 16–17
  good-quality, hallmarks of, 89–90
  hardware, 41, 89–90, 124

height of, 91
information resources, 145
inside finish, 89
kitchen size and, 19
laminate, 87–88, 122
in L-shaped kitchens, 17, 18
manufacturers of, 94
NKBA design guidelines, 19–20, 41
pantry, 92–93
stock, 33, 81–82
styles, 85
thermofoil, 88
toekick space, 92
wood, finishes for, 86–87
wood and wood veneer, 85–87
ceramic tile
for backsplashes, 126–127
for countertops, 33, 61
decorating with, 126–127
for flooring, 61–62, 127
hardness ratings of, 62
Certified Kitchen Designers, 135–136
chlorofluorocarbons, banning of, 102
collections, displaying, 128–129
colors, 42, 43
emotional responses to, 125
of laminates, 58
maintenance requirements and, 123
color scheme, choosing, 124–125
composting, 53–54, 93
computer software, for kitchen floor plan
design, 139
contractors
acting as own, 30–31
getting bids from, 33
shopping for, 30
cooking appliances. See also cooktops;
microwave ovens; ovens

ceramic glass cooktops, 109
choices available, 106–111
commercially styled adaptations, 111–114
considerations in choosing, 104, 106–111
grills, indoor, 110–111
NKBA design guidelines on, 111
placement of, 111
thermal convection, 107
cooktops, electric, 50, 106–111
ceramic glass, 109
induction cooking system, 109
magnetic induction, 39
ventilation systems, 78–79
cooktops, gas, 50, 106–107, 110
advantages of, 106, 107
ventilation systems, 78–79
costs, 25–35. See also budget
acquainting self with, 29–30
of adaptations for accessibility, 43
of appliances, 35
average, of kitchen remodels, 26–27
of cabinetry, 35, 81
of ceramic tile, 62
compromise and, 28–29
cutting, methods of, 33–35
expected, guidelines for, 28–29, 34–35
financing, 27–28
of hardwood flooring, 65
of labor, 31–32
of laminate, 58, 59
of laundry equipment, 119
of operating appliances, 95
of sinks, 60, 70
of solid-surfacing materials, 61
variability of, 25–26, 28–29, 34–35
of vinyl flooring, 64
countertops, 57–59, 61–64
butcher-block, 62–63

ceramic tile, 61
cost considerations, 58
cutting costs on, 33
durability and ease of maintenance, 57–58
heights, 20, 21, 42–43
laminate, 73
NKBA design guidelines, 20, 39, 42–43
personalizing, 126, 127
solid-surfacing materials, 59, 61, 73
surface materials, 42, 57–59, 61–64
usable frontage, NKBA guidelines for, 18

decorating schemes
    contemporary, 122, 123
    inspiration for, 129
    personalizing, 121–130
    personal preferences, 121–130
designers, professional
    budget and, 32, 131–132
    fees, 135
    finding, 133–134
    interviewing, 134
    with specialized kitchen design training,
        132–133, 135–136
    staying within budget and, 134–135
    types of, 135–138
    using to ensure accessible design, 38
    value of, 32
    working with, 131–143
desks, kitchen, 21, 93
dining areas, space planning guidelines, 18
dishwashers, 97–99
    accessibility of, 40
    considerations in choosing, 98–99
    counter space near, 39
    energy and water use, 98
    placement of, 99–100
    water use, 49–50

door handles, accessible design of, 39–40

efficiency, and kitchen layout, 15–19, 38
energy use, of appliances, 45, 47–48, 95–96,
        98, 117, 118–119
environmental protection, 45–56

faucets
    accessible design, 39–40
    flow-restricted, 55
flooring, 57–58, 64–65
    ceramic tile, 61–62, 127
    durability and ease of maintenance,
        57–58
    hardwood, 64–65, 126
    laminate, 59
    personalizing, 126
    vinyl, 64, 65, 127
floor plans. See also layout of kitchen space
    computer software for layout of, 139
    templates of, 24
food waste disposers, 54–55
functionality, and kitchen layout, 15–19

galley kitchens, 16–17
garbage disposal, 51–55, 93
granite, for countertops and floors, 64
greenhouse windows, 126
grill units, indoor, 110
G-shaped kitchen layout, work triangles in,
        18–19

hardware styles, 127–128
hardwood, for flooring, 64–65

information resources, 145–147
Interior Designers of Canada, 136, 146

International Society of Interior Designers, 136

Remodeling (magazine), 26–27

islands, 17, 21

kitchen
    defining, in planning stage, 141–143
    functions of, in lifestyle, 141–143

Kitchen Cabinet Manufacturers Association, 83

kitchen design. *See also* layout of kitchen space
    accessibility and, 38
    avoiding pitfalls of, 133
    information resources, 145–147
    integration of new technologies into, 14
    NKBA design guidelines, 14–19, 38–39
    not skimping on, 32
    planning, 15–22
    testing your knowledge of, 138–140

kitchen size
    average, 20
    cabinets and, 19

labor costs, 30–31

laminates
    for cabinetry, 87–89, 122, 123
    for countertops, 33, 58–59
    for flooring, 59

laundry equipment, 116–119
    accessibility of, 41
    energy use, 117, 118–119
    placement of, 116–117

layout of kitchen space. *See also* kitchen design; traffic flow
    categories of, 16–19

    computer software for, 139
    creating template of, 24
    galley layout, 16–17
    G-shaped layout, 18–19
    L-shaped layout, 17–18
    U-shaped layout, 18–19, 38

lifestyle, 3–11
    in determining spending priorities, 29
    functions of kitchen and, 141–143
    meaning of, 3–4
    planning process and, 3–5, 11
    questionnaire regarding, 5–11, 122–123

lighting, 34, 67, 74–77
    accessibility and, 43
    ambient, defined, 76
    compact fluorescent, 50
    fluorescent, color-corrected, 75
    halogen, 75–76
    incandescent, 75
    information resources, 146
    mood, 76
    natural, 50, 77
    NKBA design guidelines, 50, 77
    planning of, 74
    task, 76

lighting designers, professional, 75

limestone countertops and floors, 64

L-shaped kitchen layout, 17–18

magazines, home-decorating, 2–3, 133

marble, for countertops and floors, 64

microwave ovens
    accessible design, 39
    life expectancy, 115–116
    options in choosing, 115–116
    placement of, 116